Exploring the Feminine Face of God

A Prayerful Journey

Bridget Mary Meehan, S.S.C.

Sheed & Ward

Sheed & Ward™ is a service of National Catholic Reporter Publishing Company, Inc.

Library of Congress Catalog Card Number: 91-61106

ISBN: 1-55612-454-6

Published by: Sheed & Ward
115 E. Armour Blvd. P.O. Box 419492
Kansas City, MO 64141-6492

To order, call: (800) 333-7373

Contents

Acknowledgements

It is with deep gratitude that I thank my family and friends for their support in writing this book. I am grateful to my parents Jack and Bridie Meehan, my aunt, Molly McCarthy, my brothers and sisters-in-law, Patrick and Valerie, Sean and Nancy, my niece Katie, who for me is a living embodiment of the feminine face of God. I am indebted to Nancy, mother of Katie, for her descriptions of pregnancy and birth.

I also wish to acknowledge those women whose personal reflections on the feminine face of God also appear in the pages of this book. They bring a fuller imaging of God to the Christian tradition: Miriam Therese Winter, Meinrad Craighead, Joyce Rupp, Alla Renée Bozarth, Sonya Quitslund, Christin Lore Weber, Barbel Von Wartenberg-Potter, Regina Madonna Oliver, Sara Muenster. I am grateful also to Georgia Keightley for the theological framework and insights she provides in the preface. Special recognition and appreciation belongs to Marie-Celeste Fadden, O.C.D., whose drawings reflect the beauty and power of the feminine face of God.

I thank the members of my religious community, the Society of the Sisters for the Church, who have been role models and mentors for me. I wish to express particular thanks to Irene Marshall, Peg Thompson, Ana Minassian, Ron Whalen, Kathy Maquire, Roseanne Fedorko, Mary Kay Salomone, Daisy Sullivan, Dodi Granofsky, the Rev. Philip and Mrs. Cathy Duncan, Diane Pons, Maria Billick, John Weyand, Walter Montondon, Patricia Herlihy, Joseph Mulqueen, Francis Keefe, Doris Mason, Bob Schaaf, Sandy Voelker, Charles McDonnell, Mary Cashmen, Bruce Burslie, Millie Nash, Anita Eggert, Peter and Julianne Reynierse, Monika Etsell, Elizabeth Hoisington, Fritz Warren, Cheryl Sandoval, Shelly Lindell, Donna Mogan, Larry Skummer, Vlasta Messany, Helen Pickrel, Maria Kemp, Debbie Dubuque, Mary and Richard Guertin, Lola Stapels, Helen Groff, Mary Jo Grotenrath, Diane Doucette, Doc Wempe, Phil Ackers, Phil Stewart, Bob Bowen and Kaye Brown, who have been sources of inspiration and encouragement to me in my discovery of the feminine face of God.

I am deeply indebted to Regina Madonna Oliver, S.S.C., who listened, questioned and offered a comprehensive critique of each reflection in this book. I can never repay Carol and Ray Buchanan for the many hours they spent typing and collating this book for publication. Finally, I shall always be grateful to Robert Heyer, editor of Sheed & Ward, and Andy Apathy, production manager, for the production and publication of *Exploring the Feminine Face of God*.

To Mary, Mother of Jesus and Mother of the Church,
Image of the Feminine Face of God

To my mother, Bridie Meehan,
Image of the Feminine Face of God

To all women,
Images of the Feminine Face of God

Preface

That all human effort must inevitably, ultimately, fall short in the attempt to speak about the divine reality is an axiom, a precondition even, of Christian theology. And, concerning the language we *do* use—capable nonetheless of real reference to God because of the certain resemblance of creatures to their creator, as Aquinas explains—it has consistently been understood that this ever runs the risk of becoming anthropomorphic, of lapsing into the univocal.

In recognition of such, theologian Elizabeth Johnson has perceptively argued that "the very incomprehensibility of God demands a proliferation of images and a variety of names, each of which acts as a corrective against the tendency of any one to become reified and literal."[1] She goes on to make this rather pointed observation: "Normative conceptualization of God in analogy with male reality alone is the equivalent of the graven image, a finite representation being taken for and worshiped as the whole."[2] For this reason then, Johnson cites the considerable values of the present interest in and resort to the feminine analogy for God by contemporary theologians. Thematization of such novel images and concepts can not help but "disclose the relative character of male images and bracingly restrict their claim to ultimacy."[3] But even more importantly, she argues, exploration of the feminine is also indispensable for bringing to light the fullness of what it means for all of us to have been created in God's image and likeness.

The present volume represents a deliberate attempt to restore some balance to current thinking about God. Here some of the feminine images readily available in both scripture and tradition—albeit ones too little known and whose meaning has scarcely been pondered or developed—are reclaimed and made available for prayer and meditation. Here the reader is provided an alternate set of images for envisioning the divine, but especially is this imagery intended to enable the discovery—and appreciation of—God as feminine.

---

1. Elizabeth A. Johnson, C.S.J., "The Incomprehensibility of God and the Image of God Male and Female," *Theological Studies* 45 (1984): 444.

2. Ibid., p. 443.

3. Ibid., p. 444.

The author guides the reader to imagine the motherhood of God in all its contours and richness. For instance, one is encouraged to place in one's mind's eye the vision of God as a woman literally pregnant with anticipation, as the panting woman laboring, straining with excitement to bring forth the new life that has gradually taken shape within her. In another place we are invited to consider God as the watchful, ever-alert midwife for whom witness to the birth event, while something of an everyday occurrence, still never seems to lose its character of the miraculous. Yet another text calls us to realize in God the patience of the nursing mother, who in this moment of quiet repose quizzically wonders what and who this little one of hers is ultimately to become. Called before the reader's view too is the playful exchange that takes place between God\Mother and the child on her lap, an activity that not only provides a moment of special intimacy but proves a source of never-ending delight as well.

Other texts are offered which portray the feminine God as a person of strength and knowledge, as an imaginative craftswoman capable of giving shape to a vision, as a person of courage who earnestly seeks after peace, and yet for whom the practice of justice is also a virtue to be prized—all of these, of course, are attributes which characterize the biblical *Sophia*. Finally there are other texts that, taking for granted woman's experience itself is a genuine *locus theologicus*, seek to expand our awareness of and even provide new opportunities for teasing out, for discerning the feminine in God. Thus Part Four attends to the spiritual reflections of some contemporary women, highlighting their careful efforts to specify the character of God's feminine love as they have known and expressed it in the different idioms of art, poetry, and a theory of Christian ministry.

In short, this book proposes to be an exercise in plumbing "the depths of God's love as this has been revealed in feminine images." The reader's spirit can not help but be enriched by participating in such a challenging journey!

Georgia Masters Keightley, Ph.D.
Systematic Theologian
Trinity College
Washington, DC 20017

Introduction

What is God like? Can we speak of God in female as well as male terms? These are questions that people have asked through the ages. God, Yahweh, gave the people in the Hebrew Scriptures an intimation in the "I am who am" revelation of Exodus 3:14. Martin Buber translates this divine revelation to Moses as: "I shall be there as the one who will be there." To cite an exegetical discussion by Suzanne de Dietrich, this may be enlarged to encompass a nurturing connotation: "I shall be there for you. I shall remain the one whom you can experience, the one who acts, the one who comes to meet you."

The God of the Bible reveals him/herself as the one who promises to be there for us. There are no theological definitions given here out of which we may shape an idol. The second commandment, "You shall not make a carved image for yourself," warns against idol-making, shaping God according to human image. God is transcendent beyond human comprehension, and any image we may use will have a limiting effect.

Beyond our wildest imagination is God's encompassing of the totality of every good and perfect quality! Human language may attempt to gain insight into God through metaphor, but this will always fall short. Every metaphor strikes our human intuitive awareness-level as, amazingly, both true and false of God. Yes, it is true that God's love for me is a mother's warm, unconditional embrace. But it is, simultaneously, false; for I perceive that God is so much more, that the original insight is dwarfed in the face of God's magnitude. This is one basis for the growth in our time of the apaphatic mode of prayer, which abandons any attempt of the intellect to grapple with the divine through images and adopts an imageless stance, centering and resting in the Divine Presence.

Yet, the Judaeo-Christian tradition of the West has always expressed its experience of God in human images and concepts. It has used language, images and concepts to describe the Divine Presence that include both masculine and feminine qualities. However, the masculine metaphors have been in preponderance, due to the world's overtly male orientation.

The Bible uses a variety of masculine and feminine images to describe the experiences of God's people with the Holy One in their midst: God is like a loving father, a courageous warrior, a good shepherd, a mighty king, a passionate lover. But, God is also a mother eagle, a woman in labor, a midwife delivering a baby, a nurturing mother feeding her suckling infant at the breast. The Wisdom of God in the Hebrew Scriptures is the feminine personification, Sophia. Unfortunately these feminine metaphors have been relatively unexplored, until recently. The women's movement and the publications of feminist theologians have only begun to catch the public's ear, and the richness contained in prayerfully exploring these feminine metaphors is only in its initial stage of sparking the imagination and raising consciousness. The impact of a fuller imaging of God and the naming of this experience empowers, transforms and heals both women and men. "As women reimagine that which is feminine as being inclusive of strength, purpose, and personhood," Bernice Marie-Daly observes, "men conversely are reimagining that which is masculine as being inclusive of intimacy, vulnerability, and interdependence. No longer must women create only with their bodies; no longer must men create only with their minds. As this evolving convergence comes to term, human consciousness revisions and reimagines itself as whole and healthy—indeed, as blessing."

Sandra Schneider goes further than this in her perception of the "healing of wounds" inherent in meditation on God from the perspective of feminine images. In her 1986 Madeleva lecture she warned that "religious imaginations must be healed of wounds inflicted on men and women alike by the distorted males-only image of a patriarchal God."

In *Women at Prayer*, Mary Collins suggests a cure for our one-sided focus on a God-in-masculine-metaphor which has for centuries deprived human beings of an immense richness. She speaks of a needed "therapy of the imagination" and advises a tapping of the charisma of the "imaginatively gifted, who may have the resources for healing the psychic damage which is blocking living faith."

Today there is a new awareness emerging among women and men in our modern world that sexual equality and mutuality are the relational order presented by Jesus and the writers of the New Testament. This vision re-introduces the feminine face of God presented in Scripture, tradition and in mystical writings throughout the ages. There is a growing contemporary phenomenon evident in the widespread interest of the feminist movement in spirituality and in the actuality of women affirming their worth and dignity as divine images created in the divine image. The process of naming and reimaging God, using feminine images in addition to the traditional masculine ones, gives us endless possibilities for deepening our spiritual lives, and presents us with new hope for growth in wholeness and holiness. It challenges us to discover our self-image and our identity in the cosmos as human persons, women and men, called to equality and mutuality, sharing a sacred connectedness with creation.

One can assert that if the symbol system that patriarchy has given us of a male God is changed, our worldview could be radically altered. As we reimagine our divine beginning, we can incorporate a symbol system that reflects the feminine Divine and the experience of women as images of the Divine Presence. This will help all of us, women and men, to discover the beautiful dimension of the feminine and work toward a more balanced, integrated approach to spirituality and ministry.

This book is intended for women and men who are open to a new encounter with God and are prepared to journey into what will be for some uncharted waters, to plumb the depths of God's infinite love revealed in feminine images of God. *Exploring the Feminine Face of God* provides the imaginative reader with a hands-on approach of "praying with" and "reflecting on" different images of the Divine feminine in Scriptures, the mystics and contemporary writings. It presents a creative approach to discovering the transforming power of women's spirituality through this reflection. The reader is invited to trust his/her own experience of God, and become a participator in a process involving prayerful reflection, journaling and sharing with others, as she/he seeks to contemplate the richness of feminine metaphors for the Holy One, in whose image all of us have been created. Women and men will find in this experience a new opportunity to reflect upon the Divine Feminine, and to articulate the wisdom of their spiritual experiences through a variety of approaches: story, poetry, song, dance and journaling. Each chapter begins with a quote from scripture, the mystics or a contemporary author which presents God from a feminine perspective. After each reflection a series of meditative steps is provided to help the reader enter into a mode of prayerful engagement with the image. Pray this book in a relaxed manner, noticing those feelings and insights that seem to reveal a new or exciting aspect of the feminine face of God. You may choose to use these meditations in order, or to skip around as your preference dictates, reflecting on one that interests or challenges you. Be open and receptive to any opportunity for the spiritual growth your reflections may bring. God may have some wonderful surprises in store for you as you explore the feminine images of God. This book also provides food for thought for spiritual development groups, who may use it as a basis for mutual sharing and enrichment. Before coming together to discuss the book as a group, I suggest that each participant reflect on an image of God selected for the discussion. The group can then choose to do the prayer reflection either individually followed by a discussion or as a group prayer exercise. Some groups may wish to experiment by alternating these two approaches. It is in the sharing phase that each member has the opportunity to be enriched by the insights of other participants. By exploring together the feminine face of God, the community of faith creates a fuller corporate imaging of God. As communities reimagine God, I believe that they will discover new ways to internalize a feminine consciousness in powerful images that reveal our cosmic connectedness and cosmic responsibilities. For in the beginning, we were in harmony with all of creation and we delighted in who we were, male- and female-created in God's image.

Image of God's Motherly Womb Love in Scripture

Part One

Image of God's Motherly Womb Love in Scripture

The importance of feminine images in the Bible are gaining more and more interest today. In the Hebrew Scriptures the prevailing symbol is the maternal womb, the reflection of divine compassion. The Hebrew translation of this image is gratuitous love, mercy, which creates, satisfies and comforts as a mother who tenderly brings forth life from her womb, nurtures her child's growth and forgives her child's failures. This concept does not exclude fatherly love but expands our consciousness by including feminine images to describe God's presence in our lives. Even though we know that all human metaphors fall short in describing the Divine One in our midst, I believe that reflecting on God's motherly womb love in the Scriptures can reveal to us a new and rich experience of God's compassionate, tender, love that will enrich each of us on our journey to wholeness and holiness.

God A Woman in Labor   Isaiah 42:14   Marie-Celeste. OCD.

God, a Woman in Labor

Scripture Image

I have looked away, and kept silence,
I have said nothing, holding
myself in;
But now, I cry out as a woman in
labor,
gasping and panting.

Isaiah 42:14

Prayer Reflection

1. Sit or lie down comfortably in a quiet place.

2. Let go of any outside noise and distractions.

3. Close your eyes and become aware of your breathing. Inhale gently; exhale gently.

4. Spend at least several minutes focusing on the rhythm and pace of your breathing.

5. Imagine God as a woman in labor, gasping, panting, uncomfortable as the time draws near for her to give birth.

6. Enter into her pain with your whole being. Hear the cry that becomes a scream as the contractions come. . . .

7. God is breathing rhythmically and deeply getting ready for and panting as she enters into each contraction. . . .

8. Be aware of any images, feelings, thoughts, insights you are experiencing as you reflect on God as a woman in labor. . . .

9. Record your insights, feelings, images, thoughts in a journal in poetry, art, song, dance or in some other creative way.

God. A Woman in Labor   John 16:21   Marie-Celeste. oco

God, a Woman in Labor

Scripture Image

When a woman is in labor,
she is in anguish because
her hour has arrived; but
when she has given birth to a child,
she no longer remembers
the pain because of her joy
that a child has been born into the world.

John 16:21

Prayer Reflection

1. Talk with someone who has recently given birth, and ask her to describe her experience.

2. Listen to her description with your entire being: mind, senses, feelings, and intuition.

3. As you listened what did you learn about the birth process?

4. Reflect on one experience of birth that has recently occurred in your life. What did this experience reveal to you about your innermost self? your vulnerability? your strength? your courage? your patience?

5. How did this birth experience contribute to your spiritual growth?

6. Can you share these feelings and thoughts with God? with others? with nature? with the cosmos?

7. Record and celebrate your thoughts, insights and feelings through one or several of the following ways: journal, art, poetry, dance or in any creative way.

The Womb of God   Job 38:8   (The endless Sea)   Marie Celeste OCD

The Womb of God

Scripture Image

And who shut within doors the sea,
when it burst forth from the womb?

Job 38:8

Prayer Reflection

1. Take several deep slow breaths and let go of any tension in your body.

2. Be aware of places in your own body where you still feel tension or tightness and breathe relaxation into these spots. If you breath into these areas, be aware of any sensations, feelings, images or memories.

3. Image the womb as a warm home where human life grows, develops and emerges.

4. Image the womb of God as the home from which the entire cosmos comes forth: sea, sun, fire, water, wind, stars, earthly creatures, human life, the entire universe.

5. Image the womb of God giving birth to all creation, to all human life, to all earth's creatures, to all natural beauty, to the entire cosmos.

6. Use all your senses to get in touch with the birthing of all of life from the cosmic womb of God.

7. What thoughts, images, feelings, sensations, memories, insights are you aware of?

8. Record your insights, feelings, thoughts, images, memories, sensations in a journal, in art, poetry, song, dance, or in any creative way you choose.

God's Womb Pain   Galatians 4:19   Marie-Céleste, O.P.

God's Womb Pain

Scripture Image

My children,
for whom I am again in labor
until Christ be formed
in you!

Galatians 4:19

Prayer Reflection

1. Paul tells us that he will have to suffer birth pains until the image of Christ is formed within the Galatians.

2. Reflect on ways you can labor to form the Christ-image in self and in others.

3. Can you recall a time in which you did affirm the Christ-image in self and in others?

4. Can you remember a time in which you failed to affirm the Christ-image in self and in others?

5. Have you ever witnessed new life coming out of a difficult situation or painful relationship in your own life? If so, how did you feel?

6. Have you ever helped to bring about new life in a difficult situation or painful relationship for another person or persons? If so, how did you feel?

7. Is God's womb pain a helpful image to you in understanding the pain and struggle involved in your human and spiritual growth?

8. Record your insights, feelings, thoughts, sensations, memories in a journal, in art, poetry, song, dance or in any creative way you choose.

9

God Who Gave Birth to Humanity   Deut. 32:18.   Marie-Céleste, OCD

God Who Gave Birth to Humanity

Scripture Image

You were unmindful of the Rock that begot you,
*   You forgot the God who gave you birth.*

Deuteronomy 32:18

Prayer Reflection

1. Sit in a comfortable position, focusing on your breathing, and concentrating on relaxing.

2. With your eyes closed and your body relaxed, get in touch with your own spiritual journey from its very beginning, i.e., from your birth onward. Reflect on the different stages of the journey, each with its special circumstances, events and relationships. Do not focus on one stage but simply view each of them as if they were on a television screen before you.

3. Open your eyes and write down the life stages of your spiritual journey, beginning at the time you were born up to the present. Write down a phrase, sentence, or an image for each.

4. When you complete writing these, spend a few moments reflecting on the feelings, images, insights that you become conscious of. Choose a symbol or an image to represent each stage. You may wish to express your symbol through some art or poetic form.

5. During your life's journey were you aware of God's presence: Did you experience the God of love giving you birth at each new stage?

6. Does this image of God giving you birth in all the events, relationships, and circumstances of your life provide a new way of appreciating God's loving presence? Does this image open you up to a deeper understanding of God's divine concern for all humanity?

7. What thoughts, feelings, images, insights, memories, and sensations does the God who gives birth to humanity stir within you?

8. Record your thoughts, feelings, images, insights, memories, and sensations in a journal, in art, poetry, song, dance, or in any creative way you choose.

God A Comforting Mother   Isaiah 66:11,13   Marie-Céleste, OCD

God, a Comforting Mother

Scripture Image

Oh, that you may suck fully
  of the milk of her comfort,
That you may nurse with delight
  at her abundant breasts!
As nurslings, you shall be carried in her arms,
  and fondled in her lap;
As a mother comforts her [child],
  so will I comfort you;
  in Jerusalem, you shall find your comfort.

Isaiah 66:11, 12

Prayer Reflection

1. Take a few minutes to relax your body by breathing deeply. Gently, journey to the center of your being where your "inner child" dwells.

2. Get in touch with this "inner child," the part of you that wants to play, grow, wonder, delight in self, others, and in all of creation.

3. Image God as a comforting mother holding your "inner child" close to her breasts. . . .

4. Allow God to caress you . . . hold you in her lap . . . play with you . . . delight in you . . . nurture you . . . marvel with you over the splendors of creation . . . comfort you in your losses and pain.

5. How does God as comforting mother minister to the needs of your inner child?

6. How does God as comforting mother challenge you to minister to the needs of family, friends, the poor, the world?

7. What thoughts, feelings, images, memories and sensations does God as comforting mother stir within you?

8. Record your insights, feelings, thoughts, images, memories, sensations in a journal, in art, poetry, song, dance, or in any creative way you choose.

God A Nurturing Mother   Isaiah 49:15   Marie-Céleste, O.C.D.

God, a Nurturing Mother

Scripture Image

Can a mother forget her infant,
  be without tenderness for the child of her womb?
Even should she forget,
  I will never forget you.

Isaiah 49:15

Prayer Reflection

1. Take a few minutes to relax and become centered.

2. The biblical writers chose the image of a woman giving birth to help us understand the profound wonder of God's intimate love.

3. Each of us throughout our lives is enveloped in boundless love by God as an infant is enfolded within his/her mother's womb.

4. Imagine yourself as an infant floating in your mother's womb . . . free of all anxieties . . . surrounded by a warm love that permeates every fiber of your tiny body . . . nourished by the food from your mother's body . . . comforted by the steady beat of your mother's heart. . . .

5. What thoughts, feelings, images, sensations do you experience in your mother's womb?

6. Imagine yourself as an infant in the womb of God enveloped by a warm and tender love. . . . Float in the depths of Love's eternal embrace . . . listen to the heartbeat of God, your nurturing mother . . . .

7. What thoughts, feelings, images, sensations do you experience in God's womb?

8. Record your insights, feelings, thoughts, sensations, memories in a journal, in art, poetry, song, dance or in any creative way you choose.

God: A Midwife   Psalm 22: 9-10   Marie-Celeste, O.C.D.

God: A Midwife

Scripture Image

Yet you drew me out of the womb,
you entrusted me to my mother's breasts,
placed me on your lap from my birth,
from my mother's womb you have been my God.

Psalm 22:9-10 (The Jerusalem Bible)

Prayer Reflection

1. Imagine that you are a midwife assisting a woman about to give birth.

2. Look at the mother carefully. Does she appear relaxed? Is her breathing slow and rhythmic?

3. During the long hours of labor you spend your time alternating between the following activities: rubbing the mother's back, giving her verbal encouragement, using creative imagery exercises and practicing different breathing techniques.

4. As you enter the final stage of labor, you prepare the mother for the birth of her baby by encouraging her to imagine herself opening for the baby as a beautiful rose bud opens petal by petal until it is in full bloom.

5. You let her know when you first see the baby's head in the birth outlet. When the head crowns, that is when the largest diameter of the head passes through the birth outlet, you encourage her to blow through pursed lips to avoid bearing down.

6. You guide the baby's head and gently catch the slippery wet body as it comes out of the mother's womb. You immediately place the newborn infant in the mother's arms.

7. You gaze in awe at the beauty of this new life. You thank God for the role you played in helping to deliver this child.

8. Now imagine God as a midwife lovingly drawing you out of the womb and placing you at your mother's breasts.

9. What thoughts, feelings, insights, images, memories, sensations does God as midwife stir within you?

10. Record your insights, feelings, thoughts, images, memories, sensations in a journal, in art, poetry, song, dance, or in any creative way you choose.

17

10. What insights, feelings, images, thoughts, memories and sensations does God as Mother Hen arouse in you?

11. Record your insights, feelings, thoughts, images, memories, sensations in a journal, in art, poetry, song, dance or in any creative way you choose.

God: As Mother Hen

Scripture Image

Jerusalem, Jerusalem, you who kill the prophets
and stone those sent to you,
how many times I yearned to gather
your children together, as a hen gathers her young under her
wings, but you were unwilling!

Matthew 23:37

Prayer Reflection

1. Breathe deeply, slowly, and rhythmically in through your nose so that the abdomen rises on the in-breath and lowers as you breath out through your mouth. Spend several minutes doing this deep breathing exercise before you enter into your prayer reflection.

2. Become aware of any tense or tight muscles. Notice any discomfort or stress. . . . Become aware of the emotions you are feeling now. Feel them. . . . What joys are you feeling? . . . What feelings of affection? . . . . What anxieties are you feeling? . . . What guilts? . . . What angers? . . .

3. When you become aware of where you are right now, give yourself as you are, with all your feelings, to God.

4. Relax in silence before God's boundless love.

5. Imagine a mother hen gathering her chicks to her. Listen to the clucking of the mother hen as she places her small white and brown chicks under her soft warm wings.

6. Imagine God as a Mother Hen inviting all people to gather in her protective wings. Some people refuse and turn away. Others begin to come but because of certain obstacles on the path find it a difficult journey. Still others are running to God the Mother Hen.

7. To which one of these groups do you belong? To which one do your family, friends, neighbors, church, country, belong? Why? Have you belonged to each of these groups at different stages in your life?

8. What (if any) fears, anxieties, blockages are you conscious of that keep you, like the chicks, from gathering close to God the Mother Hen?

9. Gently, release these blocks, one by one, as you become aware of them and allow God to draw you into her protective embrace.

19

God: As Mother Eagle   Deut. 32: 11-12   Marie-Celeste, O.C.D.

God: As Mother Eagle

Scripture Image

As an eagle stirreth up her nest,
fluttereth over her young,
spreadeth abroad her wings,
taketh them, beareth them on her wings,
so the Lord alone did lead Jacob . . .

Deuteronomy 32:11-12 *(King James Version)*

Prayer Reflection

1. Be aware of your breathing . . . your breathing in and your breathing out. As you breathe in, breathe in God's infinite love for you. As you breathe out, breathe out God's strength. As you breathe in, breathe in God's tender compassion for the world. As you breathe out, breathe out God's justice.

2. Have a sense of God's strength and justice flowing through you to all people throughout the world.

3. Imagine a powerful mother eagle hovering over her nest . . . spreading her wings . . . gathering her young eaglets on her pinions for an early morning flight . . . Watch the eagle as she soars through the beautiful blue sunny sky with her young firmly aboard enjoying the crisp cool breeze and the warmth of the sun . . . .

4. Imagine God as a Mother Eagle carrying you on her wing . . . empowering you with her strength . . . giving you the courage you need to be a risk-taker . . . challenging you to change unjust situations and structures . . . liberating you from every kind of oppression . . . filling you with love. . . .

5. Imagine God as a Mother Eagle carrying all people on her wing . . . empowering all with her strength . . . giving all the courage to be risk-takers . . . challenging all to change unjust situations and structures . . . liberating all from every kind of oppression . . . filling all with love. . . .

6. What insights, feelings, thoughts, images, sensations, memories do you experience as you reflect on God as Mother Eagle?

7. Record your insights, feelings, thoughts, images, sensations, memories in a journal, in art, poetry, song, dance or in any creative way you choose.

Sophia: Image of God's assertive, Dynamic, Creative Love   Marie Celeste, O.C.D.

Part Two

Sophia, God as Image of Assertive, Dynamic, Creative Love

In both the Hebrew and Greek languages, Wisdom is feminine, the feminine aspect of the one God, and is personified as a woman. According to some contemporary scholars, *Sophia,* the Greek word for woman, is the better choice for reference to a person, since the English 'wisdom' tends to connote an abstract mental quality. The former, they claim, is the intention of the Biblical writers.

Sophia is a significant symbol for modern women because she portrays the assertive, dynamic feminine who believes in mutuality and plays an active role in the creation of the world and the promotion of justice and peace. Sophia sings the praises of mutuality and justice: "I love those who love me . . ./ I walk in the way of virtue/ in the paths of justice,/ enriching those who love me,/ filling their treasuries." *(Proverbs 8:17 and 20-21)*

Source: Susan Cady, Marian Ronan, Hal Taussig, *Sophia: The Future of Feminist Spirituality* San Francisco: Harper & Row, 1986, pp. 17-18.

Sophia: Woman of Strength and Knowledge: Wisdom, 8:34 Marie-Celeste
OCD

Sophia:
Woman of Strength and Knowledge

Scripture Image

She deploys her strength from one end of the earth to the
other,
>*ordering all things for good . . .*
>>*Her closeness to God lends luster to her noble birth,*
>>*since the Lord of all has loved her.*
>>>*Yes, she is an initiate in the mysteries of God's knowledge.*
>>>*She makes choice of the works God is to do.*

Wisdom 8:34 (The Jerusalem Bible, 1966)

Prayer Reflection

1. Begin by becoming quiet.

2. Gently move to a deeper consciousness . . . breathing slowly and deeply . . . listening attentively.

3. Be aware of yourself as connected with Sophia the Source of strength and knowledge within you and within all of life.

4. What thoughts, feelings images, insights, sensations does this awareness bring?

5. Image Sophia, God's wisdom, permeating all of life with new strength and deep knowledge . . . . As you experience this happening notice the changes that occur within yourself . . . others . . . events . . . situations . . . the earth . . . all of creation . . . .

6. Look at your life now. What do you know about your own strengths that seem different? exciting? challenging? risky? What do you know about others' strengths that seem different? exciting? challenging? risky? How has Sophia transformed you, others, the cosmos with her knowledge and strength?

7. What insights, feelings, thoughts, images, memories, sensations are you conscious of?

8. Record your insights, feelings, thoughts, images, memories, sensations in a journal, in art, poetry, song, dance, or in any creative way you choose.

society? How can you foster greater harmony, peace and justice in the world?

8. As you reflect on Sophia as Advocate of Transformation, what thoughts, feelings, insights, images, memories, sensations, are you conscious of?

9. Record your insights, feelings, thoughts, images, memories, sensations in a journal, in art, poetry, song, dance or in any creative way you choose.

(Source: Translation of Wisdom found in Maria Riley, *Wisdom Seeks Her Way,* Washington, DC: Center of Concern, 1987, p. 71.)

Sophia:
Advocate of Transformation

Scripture Image

For within Sophia is a spirit intelligent, holy
unique, manifold, subtle,
active, incisive, unsullied,
lucid, invulnerable, benevolent, sharp,
irresistible, beneficent,
loving to women and men.

Wisdom 7:22

Prayer Reflection

1. Sit in a comfortable position. Close your eyes. Start to relax your body. Begin with the soles of your feet and let all the tenseness drain out . . . Relax your ankles . . . Release any tightness in the calves of your legs . . . Let go of all the tension in your thighs . . . Relax each part of the back, arms, chest neck, head . . . Feel all the tension flowing out of each of these areas of your body. Enjoy the relaxation you are feeling throughout your body.

2. Read slowly Wisdom 7:22. Become aware of Sophia's presence. Let God's wisdom hold you gently, supporting each part of you. Let yourself rest, delighting in Sophia's embrace. Ask God to reveal to you new understandings of herself . . . new insights into yourself.

3. Become aware of the world: people, nations, the earth, the environment, the oppressed, the poor. Image Sophia holding everyone and everything in the world gently, supporting each one. See each one experiencing freedom, peace, justice, love, delighting in Sophia's embrace. All are interconnected, bonded together by Sophia's love.

4. What new images of God did you experience in this reflection?

5. What insights into yourself and the world did you experience in this reflection?

6. What are some ways these images, feelings and insights can nurture your spiritual growth?

7. What have you discovered about Sophia that will help you to be an advocate of social change and transformation in church and

10. Image Sophia as Comforter who assists you to find your own identity and strength in the midst of disappointments and sorrows of your life.

11. As you reflect on your experiences what insights, feelings, thoughts, images, memories, sensations, are you conscious of?

12. Record your insights, feelings, thoughts, images, memories, sensations in a journal, in art, poetry, song, dance or in any creative way you choose.

marie-celeste OCD
Counselor and Comforter   WS. 8:9,16

Sophia:
Counselor and Comforter

Scripture Image

I therefore determined to take her to share my life,
knowing she would be my counselor in prosperity,
my comfort in cares and sorrow . . .
When I go home I shall take my ease with her,
for nothing is bitter in her company,
when life is shared with her there is no pain,
gladness only, and joy.

Wisdom 8:9, 16 (The Jerusalem Bible, 1966)

Prayer Reflection

1. Begin by spending some time relaxing and centering yourself.

2. Take a deep breath, as if you were breathing through your toes and let the breath be carried up through your feet, legs, abdomen, lungs, mouth, nose—your entire body.

3. As you breathe in, say silently, "Sophia" while taking in whatever you need from Sophia: wisdom, knowledge, strength, joy, courage, comfort, peace, love . . . etc.

4. Do you remember a time when you felt whole? . . . peaceful? . . . strong? . . . joyful? . . . loving? . . .

5. Do you remember a time when you felt alienated? . . . broken? . . . hurt? . . . angry? . . . lonely? . . . guilty? . . .

6. How did you feel? What was it like? Why were these experiences significant for you? How have these experiences continued to influence you?

7. Did you discover God's comfort and /or God's counsel in any new way because of these experiences?

8. As you reflect on these experiences now, what new images of God emerge?

9. Image Sophia, God's Wisdom, as Counselor, wise guide who helps you discover meaning in your experiences and aids you in recognizing these experiences as important touchstones of your unique spirituality.

Sophia: Image of God's Goodness and Glory Wisdom 7:25,26
Marie Celeste O.D.

Sophia:
Image of God's Goodness and Glory

Scripture Image

For she is the breath of God's power
and a stream of pure glory of the Almighty.
This is why nothing polluted enters her.
For she radiates the everlasting light.
She mirrors God's energy completely,
and she images God's goodness.

Wisdom 7:25-26 (Translation of this passage is found in *Sophia: The Future of Feminist Spirituality* by Susan Cady, Marian Ronan, and Hal Taussig, San Francisco: Harper and Row, 1986, p. 33. It is from the Greek and by Hal Taussig)

Prayer Reflection

1. Be aware of any tension areas in your body. Release the tension by tensing up a given muscle and then relaxing it or by rotating your jaw or other joints. As you inhale, breathe in God's power. As you exhale, breathe out God's glory. Repeat this for several minutes or as long as it takes to become relaxed and refreshed.

2. Choose one or several of the following images for prayerful reflection:

Sophia as the breath of God's power . . .
Sophia as a stream of pure glory of the Almighty . . .
Sophia as a radiator of everlasting light . . .
Sophia as a mirror of God's energy . . .
Sophia as an image of God's goodness . . .

3. As you reflect on these images, how did you feel? Did one image appeal to you more than others? Why?

4. Did you discover God's beauty, glory, power, goodness in any new way because of your reflection on these images of Sophia?

5. If so, how do these insights bring fresh understanding to your sense of God's goodness and glory in your life.

6. As you reflected on these images, what feelings, insights, thoughts, memories, sensations were you conscious of?

7. Record your insights, feelings, thoughts, images, memories, sensations in a journal in art, poetry, song, dance, or in any creative way you choose.

7. Sophia calls us in this passage to care for the world in which we live. Think about ways you can respond to Sophia's invitation for greater involvement in the world.

8. Do you experience your work as one way in which you can contribute to human progress? What are some other ways in which you can use your gifts to enhance life?

9. What thoughts, images, insights, feelings would you want to share as an expression of your love for Sophia and for the world?

10. What thoughts, images, insights, feelings would you want to share of Sophia as Mother? . . . Sophia as Lover? . . . Sophia as Teacher? . . .

11. Record your insights, feelings, thoughts, images, memories, sensations in a journal, in art, poetry, song, dance or in any creative way you choose.

Marie-Celeste, O.C.D.

Sophia: As Mother, Lover, Teacher   Ecclesiastics 4: 11-18

Sophia: Mother, Lover, Teacher

Scripture Image

[Sophia] brings up her children
and cares for those who seek her,
Whoever loves her loves life,
those who wait on her early will be filled with happiness.
Whoever holds her close will inherit honor,
and wherever they walk the Lord will bless them.
Those who serve [Sophia] minister to the Holy One,
and the Lord loves those who love her.

Whoever obeys her judges aright,
and whoever pays attention to her dwells secure.
If they trust themselves to [Sophia], they will inherit her,
and their descendants will remain in possession of her;
for though [Sophia] takes them at first through winding
ways, bringing fear and faintness to them,
Plaguing them with her discipline until she can
trust them, and testing them with her ordeals,
in the end [Sophia] will lead them back to the
straight road, and reveal her secrets to
them.

Ecclesiasticus 4:11-18 (The Jerusalem Bible, 1966)

Prayer Reflection

1. Sit erect. Breathe deeply and relax. Become centered. Let yourself hear Sophia call your name gently and lovingly again and again.

2. Read this passage slowly, as if it were addressed to you. When a thought, feeling or image impresses you, stop and let that thought, feeling or image develop within you. Reflect on it and apply it to your life situation. Ask yourself, "What does Sophia say to me today through this passage?"

3. Focus on one of the following images in this passage: Sophia as Mother . . . Sophia as Lover . . . Sophia as Teacher.

4. As you reflect on this image, how do you feel?

5. What new understandings of God do you experience?

6. What new images of yourself do you experience?

33

stars . . . earth . . . fire . . . water . . . plants . . . flowers . . . animals . . . human beings . . . you . . . Marvel at the interdependence and connectedness of life as she has created it. Spend as much time as you wish in awe and wonder at this beautiful scene of creation.

8. What insights, feelings, thoughts, images, memories, sensations are you conscious of?

9. Record your insights, feelings, thoughts, images, memories sensations in a journal, in art, poetry, song, dance or in any creative way you choose.

Playful Craftswoman   Proverbs 8: 27-31   Marie-Céleste, O.C.D.

Wisdom: Playful Craftswoman

Scripture Image

When God set the heavens in place, I was present,
when God drew a ring on the surface of the deep,
when God fixed the clouds above,
when God fixed fast the wells of the deep,
when God assigned the sea its limits-
and the waters will not invade the land-
when God established the foundations of the earth,

I was by God's side, a master craftswoman,
Delighting God day by day
ever at play by God's side,
at play everywhere in God's domain,
delighting to be with the children of humanity.

Proverbs 8:27-31 (Translation of this passage is from the Greek by Hal Taussig found in *Sophia: The Future of Feminist Spirituality* by Susan Cady, Marian Ronan and Hal Taussig, San Francisco: Harper and Row, 1986)

Prayer Reflection

1. Take a few minutes to relax and center yourself.

2. Playfulness and humor enhance our well-being and health. Doctors tells us that laughter and play are the best stress-reducers and healers of mind, body and spirit.

3. We know that playfulness is somewhere inside of us—sometimes all we have to do is look there and we'll find it.

4. When, where, with whom do you feel playful? Having fun, taking yourself lightly, humor, playfulness—how important are they? What are your favorite ways of relaxing?

5. Try to get in touch with the "playfulness somewhere inside of you." How does it make you feel? Does it make you more aware of your body? your feelings? your mind? What images do you have of yourself as playful?

6. Image God as the "Playful Craftswoman" spinning . . . leaping . . . swirling, jumping for joy as she dances creation into being . . .

7. Use all your senses, sight, hearing, taste touch, to enter into the unfolding drama: The Cosmic Dance of the Universe . . . Observe the "Playful Craftswoman" delighting in sun . . . moon . . .

35

Woman of Peace and Discernment   Marie-Celeste OCD
Sophia   Ecclesiastics 1:17-20

Sophia:
Woman of Peace and Discernment

Scripture Image

She fills their whole house with their heart's desire
and their storerooms with her produce . . .
The crown of [Sophia] makes peace and health flourish . . .
the Lord has showered down learning and discernment with her
and exalted the renown of those who hold her close.

Ecclesiasticus 1:17-20 (The Jerusalem Bible, 1966)

Prayer Reflection

1. Sophia is both teacher and the message which is taught. Sophia is not only someone to be attentive to, she is someone to possess.

2. Breathe slowly and consciously. Relax your body part by part, from the soles of the feet to the top of the head. Repeat slowly the word "Sophia" as you breathe in deeply. Repeat slowly the word "Peace" as you breathe out deeply.

3. As you breathe in, breathe in Sophia and image Sophia filling your heart's desires . . . giving you peace . . . health . . . learning . . . discernment. As you breathe out, breathe out Sophia's gifts: Peace . . . health . . . learning . . . discernment . . . other gifts.

4. Spend some time in quiet reflection sharing with Sophia how grateful you are for the special gifts she has given to you during this prayer time.

5. Is there a part of your life where you now experience Sophia's gifts in a new way? How would you describe Sophia's power and role in your life as a result of this prayer experience?

6. What insights, feelings, thoughts, images, memories, sensations are you conscious of?

7. Record your insights, feelings, thoughts, images, memories, sensations, in a journal, in art, poetry, song, dance or any creative way you choose.

Sophia: Woman of justice Proverbs 8:18

Sophia: Woman of Justice

Scripture Image

With me
are riches and honor,
lasting wealth and justice.

Proverbs 8:18 *(The Jerusalem Bible, 1966)*

Prayer Reflection

1. Take a few moments to quiet yourself and become centered.

2. Image Sophia as the possessor of "riches and honor, lasting wealth and justice," challenging unjust structures that keep people poor and oppressed.

3. What images, words, feelings, insights, thoughts, describe your experience of Sophia as the challenger of unjust structures and liberator of the poor and oppressed?

4. Image Sophia creating a new world where peace, justice and equality flourish.

5. What images, words, feelings, insights, thoughts, describe the new world order created by Sophia?

6. Are you comfortable with this new world? Why or why not?

7. Image yourself working with Sophia, challenging unjust structures, liberating the poor and oppressed, creating a new world where peace, justice and equality flourish.

8. What images, words, feelings, insights, thoughts emerge?

8. Are you comfortable challenging unjust structures, liberating the poor and oppressed, creating a new world where peace, justice and equality flourish? Why or why not?

9. What actions, choices, or commitments can you make now to challenge unjust structures, liberate the poor and oppressed, create a new world?

10. Record your insights, feelings, images thoughts, and decisions to "do justice" in a journal, poetry, art, song, dance or in some other creative way.

marie-Celeste ocd

Sophia: Lover of the Lord of All   Wisdom 8: 2. 3

Sophia: Lover of the Lord of All

Scripture Image

I fell in love with her beauty [says the sage].
Her closeness to God lends luster to her noble birth,
since the Lord of All has loved her.

Wisdom 8:2,3 (The Jerusalem Bible, 1966)

Prayer Reflection

1. Let go all stress or tension. Do this by alternately tensing and relaxing every muscle in your body.

2. Be still and become aware of your heartbeat. Spend some time listening and cherishing the sacred beat of your heart.

3. As you listen to your heartbeat, image yourself falling deeply in love with Sophia's beauty.

4. What feelings, images, words, insights best describe your experience of falling in love with Sophia's beauty?

5. Image yourself as a beautiful, powerful, passionate reflection of Sophia.

6. What feelings, images, words, insights, best describe your experience of being a beautiful, powerful, passionate reflection of Sophia?

7. What images of God emerge from this experience of seeing yourself as a beautiful, powerful, passionate reflection of Sophia?

8. How does your experience as woman or man influence your relationship with Sophia?

9. Record your insights, feelings, images, thoughts, in a journal, in poetry, art, song, dance or in some other creative way.

Sophia: Creator of the Universe   Ecclesiastics 24: 3-5
Marie-Celeste ocd

Sophia: Creator of the Universe

Scripture Image

I came forth from the mouth of the Most High
and I covered the earth like mist.
I had my tent in the heights
and my throne in a pillar of cloud.
Alone I encircled the vault of the sky,
and I walked on the bottom of the deeps.

Ecclesiasticus 24:3-5 (The Jerusalem Bible, 1966)

Prayer Reflection

1. Begin by relaxing and centering yourself.

2. With your eyes closed and your body relaxed, journey to your divine center where Sophia dwells.

Image Sophia in one or several of the following ways:

Sophia coming forth from the mouth of the Most High.
Sophia covering the earth like mist.
Sophia's tent in the heights.
Sophia's throne in a pillar of cloud.
Sophia encircling the vault of the sky.
Sophia walking on the bottom of the deep.

3. What thoughts, feelings, images, memories and sensations emerge?

4. Now invite Sophia, to journey with you to explore hidden treasures, look for places of new life, search for dynamic energy sources within your deepest self.

5. Be aware of any images, feelings, thoughts, insights, you experience as you go on this journey.

6. Did you find any hidden treasures, places of new life, dynamic energy, sources stirring within you?

7. What did you discover about yourself on this inward journey? about Sophia? Did any of your discoveries surprise you? encourage you? challenge you?

8. Record your insights, feelings, images, thoughts, in a journal, in poetry, art, song, dance or some other creative way.

43

Part Three

Images of God's Generative, Nurturing Love in the Christian Mystics

Holy women and men throughout the ages have experienced the feminine face of God in prayer and have given it expression in their writings. Three basic themes appear in Christian mystical literature: the feminine image of the divine is portrayed as generative and sacrificial in her generation; the feminine face of God is loving, compassionate, and tender; the Feminine Divine is nurturing and maternal. In this chapter you will encounter the following prominent mystics who used explicit and elaborate feminine imagery to describe God, and Christ: Hildegard of Bingen, Mechtild of Magdeburg, Bonaventure, Meister Eckhart, Julian of Norwich, Catherine of Siena, Teresa of Avila.

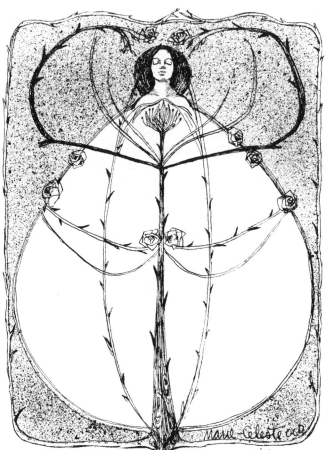

St. Bonaventure   Womb of Eternal Wisdom
"This is the wood of the Cross, on which was
hung the Salvation of the World." (chant)

St. Bonaventure (1221-1274)

Bonaventure, was born in Bagnorea, a small town in Italy. Attracted by the simplicity of St. Francis of Assisi, Bonaventure joined the Franciscan order. Famous for his intellectual ability, Bonaventure assumed the leadership of the Franciscan school in Paris. Through his gifts of diplomacy and reconciliation, Bonaventure brought unity and peace among different factions of the Franciscans, earning him the title of "Second Founder of the Franciscans." Likewise, Bonaventure was a well-known writer of medieval mystical literature and a Doctor of the Church, often referred to as "Doctor Seraphicus"—Angelic Doctor. Bonaventure used a variety of images to describe God and Christ. In his description of *The Soul's Journey into God,* Bonaventure uses the following images to describe Christ: "The way and the door," "the Mercy Seat, placed above the ark of God" and "hidden manna." Bonaventure also used feminine imagery to describe God. In the following passage Bonaventure goes beyond describing eternal wisdom as our mother. He uses the following feminine image, "the womb or uterus of eternal wisdom" . . . it "conceived them from all eternity" . . . "it produced them" . . . and "later gave birth by suffering in the flesh," to portray God's total, passionate, salvific love in conceiving, birthing, and redeeming humankind.

(Source of background information on Bonaventure: Bridget Meehan, *Nine Ways to Reach God*, Liguori: Missouri, Ligouri Publications, 1990, pp. 70-71).

"The Womb or Uterus of Eternal Wisdom"

Bonaventure writes of divine wisdom:
For all the exemplar reasons are conceived
from all eternity in the womb or uterus of
eternal wisdom . . . And as it conceived them from all eternity,
so also, it produced them or bore in time,
and later, gave birth by suffering in the flesh.

Source: St. Bonaventure, *Collations on the Six Days,* Vol. V of *The Works of Bonaventure,* trans. Jose de Vinck (Paterson, N.J.: St. Anthony Guild Press, 1970), pp301-302.

Prayer Reflection

1. Take several deep slow breaths and let go of tension in your head and neck . . . Be aware of places in your body where you feel tension or stress . . . Take several deep slow breaths and breathe relaxation into each of these areas . . . head, neck, shoulders, arms, hands, fingers, chest, stomach, pelvis, thighs, hips, knees, legs, ankles, toes.

2. Let your imagination explore the fullness of this image: "The Womb or Uterus of Eternal Wisdom." What shapes, sounds, smells, colors, and textures do you experience? Use all your senses to get a visual, textural, and audial picture. If you wish, write a description or draw a picture of this image.

3. What thoughts, feelings, sensations, insights, images emerge when you reflect on this image? Talk to God about them, one by one. Listen to God's response to you.

4. In what ways can Bonaventure's metaphor "The Womb or Uterus of Eternal Wisdom" provide a new glimpse into the mystery of God's presence? Are you comfortable with this image? Why? Why not?

5. After reflecting on "The Womb or Uterus of Eternal Wisdom," write down anything that comes to mind in words, pictures, impressions, or poetry. Read what you have written to yourself, permitting yourself to focus on the feelings, images, and impressions that come to you about what you have written.

6. If you would like, write a conversation or dialogue between you and "The Womb or Uterus of Eternal Wisdom." Address any questions or concerns, you may have about the mysteries of human life (such as: Why do good people suffer? Why does evil exist in the world? What is the meaning of human sexuality?) to "The Womb or Uterus of Eternal Wisdom." Let yourself write freely without censuring your thoughts or feelings.

7. Read what you have written in this dialogue. What thoughts, feelings, insights, sensations, images do you experience? Write down anything that you are aware of in words, pictures or impressions.

8. What does the image of womb or uterus reveal to you about human sexuality? about human spirituality? What do you know about your own sexuality from the inside? What images, feelings, sensations describe your experience of your own sexuality? What does the image of womb or uterus reveal to you about the union of sexuality and spirituality?

9. If you like, write down the important moments in your psycho-sexual-spiritual development beginning with conception up to the present. Let yourself write freely, without censuring your thoughts or feelings. Describe key moments when you became aware of your body, sexual images, sexual feelings, sexual differences, sexual messages and sexual education received from parents, church, family, society etc.

10. Read what you have written about your psycho-sexual-spiritual development, allowing yourself to focus upon the feelings, images and impressions that come to you about what you have written. Record anything that emerges in words, images and impressions.

11. Can reflecting on "The Womb or Uterus of Eternal Wisdom" enhance your appreciation of your psycho-sexual-spiritual development? If so, why? If not, why not? If you are a woman, do you find this image helpful in developing insights into your sexuality and spirituality? If you are a man, do you find this image helpful in developing insights into your sexuality and spirituality?

12. Record your insights, images, feelings, thoughts, in a journal, poetry, art, song, dance or in some other creative way.

from death portrait
marie-celeste, o.s.d.

ST. BONAVENTURE FIDANZA, O.S.F.

Meister Eckhart: The god who gives Birth

Marie Celeste, O.CD

Meister Eckhart (1260-1328)
The God Who Gives Birth

As a poet, mystic, preacher, philosopher and theologian, Meister Eckhart had a profound impact on the world of his time and continues to have a significant influence on contemporary spirituality. Witness the popularity of creation-centered spirituality today, advocated by Matthew Fox among others, which finds inspiration in Eckhart's mystical vision.

Meister Eckhart, a Dominican, lived in an age described by one author as "The Calamitous 14th century." He called for reform in a time when church and society were mired in decadence, scandal, and corruption. A spirit of despair, guilt and frustration prevailed. As a prophet and social critic, Eckhart advocated reform. He identified with the poor and oppressed of his time—with the lower class women in the Beguine movement and preached to the peasants in their own vernacular. As a result of lack of understanding on the part of church authorities, Eckhart was condemned the year after his death by papal decree.

Contemporary scholars today agree that Eckhart was unjustly condemned and that his works are orthodox. Eckhart's "this world" theology and holistic spiritual vision continue to be a touchstone for many who seek a more holistic approach to spirituality.

Eckhart speaks of God within each of us in a personal, creative and creating word. All persons and all creatures come from and image our Birther God. We discover in Eckhart an image of God as intimate, passionate birther who gives birth to God's word within us with "the kiss of the soul, there mouth comes to mouth."

(Source: Eleanor Rae and Bernice Marie Daily, *Created in Her Image*, New York: Crossroad, 1990, p. 109.)

"The property of the Father to give birth is nothing else than his being God, and I have already said that he held nothing back. And I further say that it is the very root of divinity which he full speaks into his Son."

(Source: Matthew Fox, *Breakthrough* (New York: Image Books, 1980, p. 322.)

Prayer Reflection

1. Take some time to relax your body and find a comfortable position in which to rest. Close your eyes, let go of any tension and stress. Picture yourself as a growing fetus peacefully floating in the amniotic fluid within your mother's womb. How do you feel as the time approaches for your birth? Excited? Anxious? Joyful? Hopeful?

2. Eckhart says that the core of God's divinity is the property to give birth. God's speech is a birth in itself. For God to express God is to give birth to all creatures forever creative and creating.

3. Each of us at every moment of our lives is like an infant awaiting birth. God is forever creating us in God's image. Each of us is a new word from the mouth of God. Our life situations and relationships provide us with many opportunities to experience being born and reborn. We are profoundly connected, intimate birthers of God's forgiveness, compassion, healing and love in each other's lives.

4. Review the relationships that you have now with people who are really important to you and who have loved you. Recall them one by one. How can you experience rebirth in these relationships? Be aware of opportunities you may have to be an intimate birther of God's love to others. Notice the changes that might need to occur so this can happen in each of these relationships.

5. Write down the names of several significant persons that came to mind. Choose one of them to dialogue with—perhaps someone with whom you have had a difficult relationship or someone with whom you want to develop a closer relationship.

6. Once you have selected your significant person, write a description of your relationship with this person. State both positive and negative aspects of the relationship from the beginning up to the present. Be aware of your feelings.

7. Close your eyes and imagine yourself with this person. Begin to talk to this person about your desire for reconciliation and/or a closer relationship. Listen to the other person's perspective and feelings as well as to your own. Discuss what kinds of changes need to occur before either or both of you will experience new birth in your relationship. Decide on the actions both of you will choose to do to make this rebirth a reality. Write down the conversation as it unfolds and any decisions or commitments either or both of you wish to make.

8. When you finish the dialogue, read it back to yourself and be aware of any images, feelings, insights that occurred to you.

9. Record these images, feelings, insights in a journal, poetry, art, song, dance or in some other creative way.

MEISTER ECKhart, O.P. poet, mystic

The Breast Milk of God: Interior Castle of St. Teresa of avila

Teresa of Avila (1515-1582)
The Breast Milk of God

St. Teresa of Avila was born in Spain and entered the convent of the Incarnation at Avila in 1536. Undaunted by the opposition of some in her order as well as clergy and laity, Teresa reformed the Carmelite Order, founding houses in which the Primitive Rule of the Order of Carmel would be observed. In recognition of her mystical writings and the spiritual influence Teresa exerted on people of all ages, the Church honored this "mystic reformer" with the title of "Doctor of the Church."

In her writings Teresa presents herself as a woman of passionate love for God and for people. Teresa describes prayer as a living relationship with God and her teaching discusses practical ways to prepare for this relationship; the obstacles that may arise from our human weakness, our lack of commitment and openness, and suggests approaches to overcome our blockages and resistance. Relationships with others are, according to Teresa, the indicator of our progress in prayer. "What value God places on our loving and keeping peace with one another!" (*The Way of Perfection* 36:6). Using images in her writings, such as garden, castle, fountain, and flames, Teresa describes eloquently the spiritual journey in ways that touch the hearts of people universally. In *The Interior Castle,* Teresa utilizes the nursing image of the breast milk of God to describe God's comforting love for all people.

(Source: Sister Mary, O.D.C., *Daily Reading With St. Teresa of Avila* introduction, Springfield, Illinois: Templegate Publishers, 1985, p. 19).

For from those divine breasts
where it seems God is always sustaining the soul
there flows streams of milk bringing comfort to all the people.

(Source: *The Interior Castle,* translated by Kieran Kavanaugh and Otilio Rodriguez O.D.C., New York: Paulist, 1979, pp. 179-180).

Prayer Reflection

1. Spend a few minutes in silence. Concentrate on your breathing. As you breathe in, image God's love filling every area of your body. As you breathe out, image divine love flowing through you to family, friends, co-workers, neighbors, the human family.

2. Read Teresa's words again. If a particular phrase or image touches your mind and heart, reflect on the meaning of the phrase or image for you. What is God saying to you by drawing you to this phrase or image?

3. What thoughts, feelings, sensations, insights, images emerge when you reflect on this phrase or image? Talk to God about them, one by one. Listen to God's response to you. You may find journaling this conversation helpful.

4. Close your eyes and visualize Teresa's feminine image of divine compassion—the breast milk of God flowing from the divine breasts to comfort you . . . Taste this milk . . . Let it heal your wounds . . . remove your anxieties and fears . . . satisfy your hunger and thirst for abundant life.

5. Now image the breast milk of God flowing from the divine breasts to comfort your family, friends, co-workers, the human family . . . See each one taste this milk . . . Observe the healing that occurs . . . The fears that God removes . . . The hunger and thirst for abundant life that God satisfies . . .

6. Pray for the strength to do whatever needs to be done to bring God's compassionate love to others—either in your family, in your circle of friends, at work or in the human family.

7. What actions, choices, or commitments can you make now to become a dynamic reflection of God's compassionate love for others?

8. Record your insights, images, feelings, thoughts, choices and decisions, commitments in a journal, poetry, art, song, dance or in some other creative way.

Teresa of Avila

Mechtild of Magdeburg (1210-1280)
God's Maternal Breast

Mechtild of Magdeburg was born in a small town on the Elbe River in what is now Germany. Mechtild was a member of the Beguines, a group of women who lived in community, worked for a living, but did not marry and did not become nuns. As a "mystic prophet" Mechtild spoke boldly about injustice in society and in the Church calling some of the priests "foolish layfolk" who refuse to take responsibility for church renewal. In her writing Mechtild invites us to see God as mother who "lifts her loved child from the ground to her knee." (iv, 22)* She discovers her soul in the Trinity which is like "a mother's cloak wherein the child finds a home and lays its head on the maternal breast." (vi, 7)

A contemporary of Eckhart, Mechtild describes God as mother, birther, creator. Both Mechtild and Eckhart reveal to us a birthing call, a consciousness of these births: the birth of a new self, the birth of God in ourselves, and the birth of ourselves as sons and daughters of a God who is both Mother and Father. We are called to participate in the building of the kingdom and to transform the world. "When we on earth pour out compassion and mercy from the depths of our hearts and give to the poor and dedicate our bodies to the service of the broken, to that very extent do we resemble the Holy Spirit who is a compassionate out-pouring of the Creator and the Son." (vi, 32)

God is not only fatherly.
  God is also mother
    who lifts her loved child
      from the ground to her knee.
        The Trinity is like a mother's cloak
          wherein the child finds a home
            and lays its head on the maternal breast.

---

*Each reference from Mechtild's writings has two reference numbers. The first, a Roman numeral, indicates one of her seven 'books' which constitute one volume. The second number indicates the entry number given in *The Revelation of Mechtild of Magdeburg* or *The Flowing Light of the Godhead*, trans. Lucy Menzies (London: Longmans, Green and Co., 1953).

(Source: Sue Woodruff, *Meditations With Mechtild of Magdeburg* (Sante Fe, New Mexico: Bear & Company, 1982) pp. 5-7, 11, 19-20, 109.)

Prayer Reflection

1. Relax. Let all tensions go. Concentrate on your breath. Breathe slowly. Read Mechtild's words again. Select a line that touches you. Repeat the line several times to discover its meaning. Use your imagination to explore the beautiful female imagery in depth.

2. Compose your own mantra or short prayer to help you experience God's presence in this passage. Slowly say this phrase or another of your choosing over and over again. If a distraction comes, simply ignore it. Just repeat your mantra and image yourself resting on God's maternal breast.

3. Become aware of your feelings . . . Are you experiencing any or some of the following emotions: joy . . . hope . . . affection . . . anxiety . . . fear . . . anger . . . guilt? (You may want to journal a description of your feelings).

4. Spend some time meditating on the following feminine metaphors that Mechtild uses to describe divine nurturing love:

"God is also mother who lifts her loved child from the ground to her knee" . . . "The Trinity as a maternal cloak" . . . "The child finds a home and lays its head on the maternal breast."

5. Recall times in which you nurtured other people last month. Visualize each experience. Offer a prayer of gratitude for each opportunity you had to reflect God's nurturing love to others.

6. Recall times in which you were nurtured by other people last month. Visualize each experience. Offer a prayer of thanksgiving for each person who has given you nurturing love.

7. Recall one person who needs God's nurturing love. List all the ways that you could demonstrate love for him/her. Visualize this person. Imagine yourself giving nurturing love to him/her.

8. Make a decision to do something in the next week to share nurturing love with this person.

9. Record your feelings, images, thoughts, insights, decisions in a journal, poetry, art, song, dance or in some other creative way.

Julian of Norwich
The Motherhood of God

Julian of Norwich, a fourteenth century English mystic, presents a well-developed vision of God in a complete cycle of life from before birth to after death in *Revelations of Divine Love*. What Julian develops is a description of God's mothering activity which begins with conception in the womb; the pain and trauma of labor and birth, the nurturing of the suckling child, the care, education and rotation of the older child; the bathing, healing, forgiving, guiding and comforting of the child as it grows and matures; and the continual loving attentive care of the child even to the point of its death and return to the original womb. Julian views the motherhood of God as complement to the fatherhood of God. Julian strives for an integration of all that is best of what we can conceive and experience of God. She describes the quality of a mother as present in the Trinity, as well as that of a Father, a Son and their Spirit.

For a scholarly study of Julian of Norwich see " 'God Is Our Mother': Julian of Norwich and the Medieval Image of Christian Feminine Divinity" by Jennifer Perone Heimmel, St. John's University Doctoral Dissertation, 1980; published on demand by the University Microfilms International. (I am deeply indebted to this outstanding study for background and selections for this chapter.)

Source: Heimmel abstract see below. The excerpts that follow are taken from Julian of Norwich, *Showings*. Take time to contemplate with Julian the feminine face of God!

As truly as God is our Father, so truly is God our Mother . . .
To the property of motherhood belong nature, love, wisdom
and knowledge, and this is God . . . We have our being from him
(Jesus Christ) where the foundation of motherhood begins,
with all sweet protection of love which endlessly follows . . .
The mother can give her child a suck of milk, but our
precious Mother Jesus can feed us with himself
and does . . ."

(Source: Julian of Norwich, *Showings* translated by Edmund Colledge and James Walsh from the Classics of Western Spirituality Series (New York: Paulist, 1978) pp. 293-299.

Prayer Reflection

1. Quiet yourself by looking into the glow of a burning candle. Focus your eyes on the flame. Feel yourself relax in God's warm, loving presence.

2. What thoughts, feelings, sensations, insights, images emerge when you reflect on Julian's description of the Motherhood of God as nature, love, wisdom, and knowledge?

3. What thoughts, feelings, sensations, insights, images emerge when you reflect on Julian's description of the motherly qualities of Jesus?

4. Record your thoughts, insights, feelings, images about Julian's description of Jesus' motherly qualities.

5. How can you be receptive to the compassion and tenderness of Jesus' mothering love in your life? relationships? prayer? work? play?

6. In what ways can you bring Jesus' mothering love to others? How would you feel about doing this?

7. Record your insights, feelings, images, thoughts, and decisions about being a reflection of Jesus' mothering love to others.

JULIAN OF NORWICH

MECHTILDE OF MAGDEBURG

Julian of Norwich
God Our Mother

As truly as God is our Father, so truly is God our Mother . . .
I am . . . the power and goodness of fatherhood;
I am . . . the wisdom and the lovingness of motherhood

(*Showings*, pp. 293-299.)

Prayer Reflection

1. Use the following relaxation exercise to become still. Be attentive to your body . . . Notice any areas of tension or stress . . . Become aware of your feelings . . . What anxieties, longings, fears, guilts are you feeling? . . . What joys, desires, hopes, affections are you experiencing? . . . What are some of the thoughts, insights you are pondering? . . .

Acknowledge these feelings, desires, thoughts, insights. Be still and rest in God's motherly love for you.

2. With your eyes closed and your body relaxed, get a sense of your own spiritual journey from its beginning, e.g., from your birth to today. Let your own inner wisdom reveal to you the stages of the journey, each with its own special persons, situations and events.

3. Open your eyes and write down the life stages of your spiritual journey, beginning at the time you were born up to the present time.

4. Did you experience God's mothering love during any of the life stages in your spiritual journey? What images, feelings, sensations, thoughts, insights emerge when you reflect on this experience?

5. Elaborate upon your experience, write down what kind of time it was for you, describing the persons, situations, events, feelings, thoughts, images that come to your mind.

6. When you have finished, reflect upon what you have written; then select a symbol that you feel is representative of this experience. You may choose to express your symbol through art, poetry, drama, dance or through some other creative expression.

Julian of Norwich: God's Feminine, Passionate Love
marie-celeste, OCD

Julian of Norwich
God's Feminine Passionate Love

I am . . . the light and the grace which is all blessed love . . .
I am . . . the great supreme goodness of every kind of thing;
I am . . . the one who makes you to love;
I am . . . the one who makes you to long;
I am . . . the endless fulfilling of all true desires.

(*Showings,* p. 296.)

Prayer Reflection

1. Take time to relax and be still. Select one of the lines above as a prayerful mantra. Repeat it slowly and gently and allow it to lead you on a journey of discovery into the depths of God's feminine, passionate love.

2. Imagine a ruby flame four or five feet above your head. It comes to rest upon you and encompasses your whole body centering itself in your heart.

3. This flame expands fanned by the oxygen of your love-response, filling your whole body. It burns away anxiety, resentment, depression, anger, negative hostile attitudes . . . Feel the purifying light of God's feminine passion transforming your entire being . . . enlightening you with new vision . . . energizing you with new strength . . . empowering you with a new compassionate love . . .

4. As you open yourself to God's feminine passionate love, what images, feelings, sensations, thoughts, insights emerge?

5. Imagine yourself loving everyone in your life you are called upon to love with God's feminine passionate love . . . Imagine yourself bringing a new vision of hope to the world, working with new strength to create a more just world, and loving with new compassion all creation.

6. As you see yourself being a reflection of God's feminine passionate love to the world, what images, feelings, sensations, thoughts, insights emerge?

7. Write as many sentences as you can beginning with "I am . . ." describing gifts which you possess that reflect God's feminine passionate love to others and to the world.

8. What actions, choices or commitment can you make now to become a dynamic reflection of God's feminine passionate love for others? for all creation?

9. Make a list of "I can . . . " statements sharing what you have decided to do to share God's feminine passionate love with others and with all creation.

10. Record your insights, images, feelings, thoughts and insights in a journal, poetry, art, song, dance or in some other creative way.

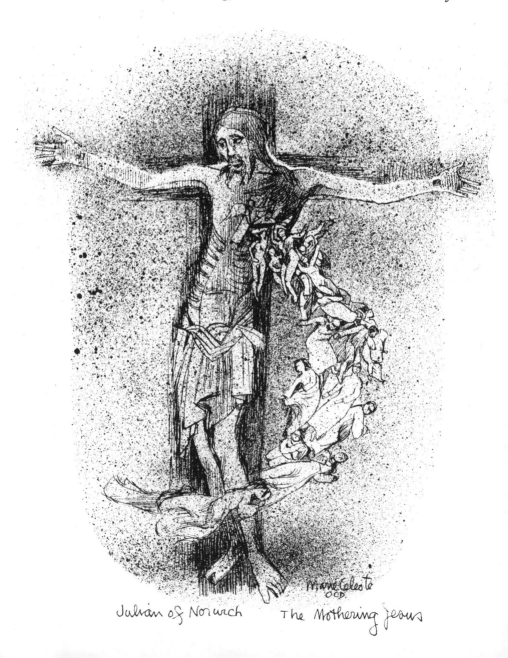

Julian of Norwich   The Mothering Jesus

Julian of Norwich
The Mothering Jesus

Scripture Image

The mother can give her child a suck of milk, but our precious
Mother Jesus can feed us with himself and does . . .
The mother can lay her child tenderly to her breast, but our
tender Mother Jesus can lead us easily into his blessed breast
through his sweet open side, and show us there a part of the
godhead and of the joys of heaven, with inner certainty of
endless bliss.

(*Showings* p. 298.)

Prayer Reflection

1. Close your eyes and call to mind an image of a nursing mother, baby in arms. Imagine yourself as a nursing infant in the arms of the mothering Jesus.

2. What thoughts, feelings, sensations, insights, images emerge when you reflect on this experience?

3. Talk to Jesus about this mothering of you. Be honest with Jesus about your feelings. Is this image difficult for you? exciting? challenging? (You may want to journal your response).

4. Reflect on the sources of stress and frustration in your life. Are there any areas in your life that need Jesus' mothering love? You may wish to list them on paper.

5. When you have finished, try to let go of each anxiety by releasing it to Jesus. To symbolize your letting go, open your hands, palms up, on your lap. As you do this imagine Jesus holding you close in a loving embrace, healing you and revealing to you the "joys of heaven."

6. Can reflecting on the Mothering Jesus put you in touch with your ability to nurture yourself? others? new ideas, visions, programs, etc.? If so why? If not, why not? If you are a woman do you find this image helpful in developing new insights into your spiritual potential? If you are a man do you find this image helpful in developing new insights into your spiritual potential?

7. Record your insights, images, feelings, thoughts in a journal, poetry, art, song, dance or in some other creative way.

Marie Celeste OCD

Hildegard of Bingen: Feminine Love Births Creation
from her 'Illuminations'

Hildegard of Bingen (1098-1179)
Feminine Love Births Creation

Hildegard, the youngest of ten children, was born in the summer of 1098 at Bickelheim and is often referred to as one of the most popular Rhineland Mystics. Hildegard had visions as a young girl and at the age of eight joined Jutta a holy anchoress to be educated in the Benedictine way of life: prayer, work, spinning, music, and Scripture. When she was eighteen, Hildegard became a Benedictine nun and in the years that followed became well-known as an artist, scientist, preacher and mystic. In 1151 Hildegard and the nuns in her community moved to a larger monastery in Rupertsburg. In their new monastery, Hildegard and her community flourished, developing their creative gifts in music, song and painting in innovative and exciting ways. Hildegard travelled and preached in the cathedrals such as Trier and Bamber, warning the archbishop, clergy and people about the corruption and abuses in the church. (Source: *Illumination of Hildegard of Bingen*, Matthew Fox, Sante Fe: New Mexico, Bear & Company, 1985, p. 6-8.)

Hildegard challenged pope and emperor alike, defied bishops, and as one writer observed: " . . . her ceaseless complaints about a society run and ruled by men, placed a special responsibility on frail creatures like herself . . . seemed to reflect a profound disillusionment with a social order which gave women few rights and no power." (Source: Bernhard W. Scholz, "Hildegard Von Bingen on the Nature of Woman," *The American Benedictine Review*, December 1980, pp. 370f.)

In 1979, Pope John Paul II, on the 800th anniversary of Hildegard's death, called her an "outstanding saint, a light to her people and her time [who] shines out more brightly today."

(Source: Joannes Paulus Pontifex II, "Pope's Letter to Cardinal Volk, Bishop of Mainz," *L'Osservatore Romano*, October 1, 1979, p. 10).

Her first book, *Scivias* (Know the Ways) contains her mystical visions and illuminations. In her illuminations Hildegard describes God birthing creation and holding all of creation in perfect harmony and balance. According to Hildegard's vision, feminine love births creation. "But why does the whole creation call this maiden 'Lady'?" Because "it was from her that all creation proceeded, since love was the first. She made everything." "Love created humankind . . . Love was in eternity and it brought forth in the beginning all holiness all creatures without any admixture of evil." (Source: Cited in text that follows.)

In a letter to Abbot Adam of Ebrach, Hildegard of Bingen (1098-1179) describes a vision in which she saw *"an extraordinarily beautiful young woman . . . wearing shoes which seemed of purest gold [whom] the whole creation called 'Lady'. The image spoke to a person pictured in sapphire blue and said: 'Dominion is yours on the day of your power in the radiance of the saints. I have brought you forth from my own womb before the daystar.'"*

Hildegard then describes hearing a voice which told her: *"The young woman whom you see is Love. She has her tent in eternity . . . For it was love which was the source of this creation in the beginning when God said: 'Let it be!' And it was. As though in the blinking of an eye, the whole creation was formed through love . . . But why does the whole creation call this maiden 'Lady'? Because it was from her that all creation proceeded, since love was the first. She made everything . . . Love created humankind . . . Love was in eternity and it brought forth in the beginning of all holiness all creatures without any admixture of evil."*

(Source: Adelgundis Fuhrkotter, transl., *Hildegard von Bingen, Briefwechsel* Salzburg: 1965, pp. 140f. In *Illuminations of Hildegard of Bingen* (text by Hildegard of Bingen with commentary by Matthew Fox, Sante Fe: New Mexico: Bear & Company, 1985, pp. 52-53)

Prayer Reflection

1. Sit with God by a river, or in the mountains, or under a tree, or some favorite place. Be aware of God's presence within you and all around you. Let the beauty of this place fill your spirit with peace.

2. Observe the color and shape of things. If you had to draw the area in which you sit, how would you do it?

3. Listen to the sounds that you hear. Could you put them together into music, song, dance?

4. Touch the texture of things around you. Be aware of how they feel.

5. Contemplate these marvels as a person-in-awe of God's creation.

6. Hildegard's vision introduces us to our loving God who passionately gives birth to all creation. Reflect on the images she uses to describe the birthing of creation:

> "Dominion is yours on the day of your power in the radiance of the saints. I have brought you forth from my own womb before the daystar."

> "God said: 'Let it be!' And it was. As though in the blinking of an eye, the whole creation was formed through love . . . But why does the whole creation call this maiden 'Lady'/ Because it was from her that all creation proceeded, since love was the first. She made everything . . . Love created humankind . . . "

7. Close your eyes and visualize Hildegard's vision of divine Love birthing creation. What images do you see? How do you feel? Are you aware of any new insights into the creative moment?

8. All creation, including human beings, image our Birther God. We are interrelated and interconnected to one another. Each of us reflects the divine image in a special way. We have a responsibility to birth one another by sharing in God's ongoing creative process in each other's lives. How can you be a birther of love, hope, justice, equality for others? for the world? In what ways do you need others to birth you?

9. What actions, choices, or commitments can you make now to become a birther of God's creative love in the lives of others? in the world? What actions, choices or commitments can you make now to open yourself to others' birthing you?

10. Record your insights, images, feelings, thoughts, choices, decisions and commitments in a journal, poetry, art, song, dance or some other creative way.

Hildegard of Bingen from her self-portrait

from painting by Pintoricchio

St. Catherine of Siena — debate with Pope on return of Papacy from Avignon to Rome.

ST. Catherine of Sienna: God as Nursing Foster Mother

St. Catherine of Siena (1347-1380)
Christ as Nursing Foster Mother

St. Catherine of Siena was born in Siena, Italy, the second youngest of twenty-five children. She consecrated her life to Christ as a Dominican tertiary at the age of sixteen. Often referred to as a "mystic activist," because of her work with the poor and her refusal to compromise the values of the gospel, Catherine advocated reform in a Church racked by social and political tension. In recognition of her role, Pope Paul VI gave her the title "Doctor of the Church" in 1970. In the *Dialogue* of St. Catherine of Siena, Catherine first uses maternal imagery of breasts and milk to describe church as spouse and mother. God, then continuing the discussion with Catherine, refers to Christ as son, physician, and finally as a nursing foster mother who cures the sick child through a selfless act of sacrifice.

Christ drinking this bitter medicine, which humankind
could not drink on account of our great weakness,
like a foster-mother who takes medicine instead of
her suckling, because she is grown up and strong,
and the child is not fit to endure its bitterness.

Christ was humankind's foster-mother, enduring,
with the greatness and strength of the Deity
united with your nature, the bitter medicine
of the painful death of the cross, to give life to you
little ones debilitated by guilt.

(Source: St. Catherine of Siena, *The Dialogue of St. Catherine of Siena,* trans. Algar Thorold. London: Kegan Paul, Trench, Trubner & Co. Ltd., 1907, pp. 68-69.)

Prayer Reflection

1. Sit in a comfortable position, focusing on the rhythm of your breathing and concentrating on being open to God.

2. With your eyes closed and your body relaxed, become conscious of the situations or events which have been obstacles or negative experiences in your spiritual journey.

3. Review the times in your life when you have felt most alienated from God and others—for instance, situations or times when you may have experienced depression or loneliness; when you felt resentment, anger, jealousy, guilt, hatred in your relationships; or when you felt grief, abandonment, loneliness, etc. Simply identify these situations allowing them to appear one by one, without examining any one in detail.

4. Open your eyes and write down as many of these events as you can remember. Use a word or phrase to describe each one.

5. Choose one about which you have strong feelings, one which may still evoke anger, guilt, bitterness, sadness, jealousy, fear, resentment, hurt, etc.

6. Once you have selected it, write about it. Describe it in as much detail as you can recall. What relationships, circumstances, activities were you involved in at the time that this event occurred?

7. Now close your eyes and imagine this event as it happened. Once you can picture it clearly and experience yourself in it, then see Christ entering this situation, embracing you tenderly. Allow yourself to become like a trusting child in Christ's arms as you share your painful feelings openly and completely, holding nothing back.

8. Picture Christ as a Nursing Foster Mother listening to you and ministering to your wounds compassionately. Observe how Christ takes the bitter medicine of your sadness and transforms it. Notice what Christ does to fill your emptiness and heal your pain. See Christ's powerful love melt your blockages and give you the courage to grow spiritually in this situation.

9. Ask Christ, your Foster Mother, for whatever you most need to grow spiritually in this situation, whatever it may be: forgiveness, freedom, healing, faith, peace, joy, hope. Picture yourself surrendering to Christ the fear, guilt, anxiety, despair, resentment, loneliness, grief, hatred, one by one. Observe the Divine Foster Mother receiving each one, redeeming each one, transforming each one by the grace of the Cross and Resurrection.

10. See yourself surrounded by the glorious presence of divine love. Allow yourself to experience Christ's healing and peace as fully as possible. Open yourself to any other gift your Nursing Foster Mother may wish to give to you at this time.

11. Open your eyes and record your insights, feelings, thoughts, images, memories, sensations in a journal, in art, poetry, song, dance, or in any creative way you choose. Be aware of what may have been surprising, enjoyable or challenging in this reflection.

Part 4

Images of God's Feminine Love: Some Reflections by Contemporary Women

Today we experience a new and powerful consciousness emerging about how we describe God. Male images of God no longer present a better or more accurate description of God than female images. Since God is both female and male and neither female nor male, there is a need for an inclusive language for God that utilizes the images and experiences of both women and men. This, I propose, can only happen by naming God in female as well as male metaphors. Part 4 presents a rich tapestry of feminine images of God that will expand awareness of and offer opportunities for integration of the feminine dimension of God's presence in our lives. In these reflections, ten contemporary women reveal some new and beautiful dimensions of the Divine Feminine Face of God. Each reflection is followed by creative suggestions for prayer and spiritual growth.

Mother Earth: The Fruit of God's Womb   Marie Celeste O.C.D.

Mother Earth: The Fruit of God's Womb

The earth was formless and empty.
  There was a darkness over the deep.
    God paused, reflected.
      Her brooding spirit hovered restlessly over the face of waters
      savoring the stillness, embracing the mystical moment,
      contemplating the indissoluble cord binding Her to the earth.
        God loved the fruit of Her womb with all its potential for good.
          Intuitively, She broke the silence, singing: Let there be light!
        Her sunlight chased the shadows.
          She danced with the moon and the stars.
            She sang all life into being: seeds, trees, fruits
            and flowers, birds that took to the heavens and
            creatures that kept to the earth.

She taught earth all about motherhood, about nature and birth.
  God sang: Let there be life fashioned in My image.
    She created humankind in Her image, rational beings
      She created them, female and male She created them, from out of
      the earth She created them.

From the humus of earth, from mud, from muck,
  She fashioned in Her image woman and man,
    breathed into them Her spirit, the very breath of life.

From the beginning humankind is the love child of
  our God in the womb of Mother Earth.

(Creation Accounts in Genesis by Miriam Therese Winter, *WomanPrayer, WomanSong,* Oak Park Illinois: Meyer Stone Books, 1987, pp. 25-26.)

Prayer Reflection

1. Take time to relax and be still. Notice your breathing in and your breathing out. Each time you breathe in, breathe in God's creative love for Mother Earth, for all earth creatures, for human persons. Each time you exhale breathe out God's creative love for Mother Earth, for all earth's creatures, for human persons. Each time you exhale breathe out God's creative love for Mother Earth, for all earth's creatures, for human persons.

2. When you become centered, imagine you are present at the dawn of creation. Read this contemporary account of creation,

slowly and reflectively, imagining God creating, loving and celebrating Mother Earth and all of life as the "fruit of Her womb." Pause as often as you wish to allow God to communicate with you in whatever way She wishes.

3. How do the following images describe the sacredness of Mother Earth as the fruit of God's womb and our interconnectedness with the earth? ". . . God paused, reflected . . . contemplating the indissoluble cord binding Her to the earth."

"God loved the fruit of Her womb with all its potential for good." "She sang all life into being: seeds, trees, fruits and flowers, birds that took to the heavens and creatures that kept to the earth."

4. As you reflect on the above description of creation, what thoughts, images, feelings, sensations, memories, insights, are you aware of?

5. Reflect on this passage using the questions that follow: "She created humankind in Her image, . . . female and male She created them, from out of the earth She created them. From the humus of the earth, from mud, from muck, She fashioned in Her image woman and man, breathed into them Her spirit, the very breath of life." How does it feel to image God the Creator of all life as a woman? What thoughts, feelings, images, insights, sensations emerge when you image a feminine God creating you in Her image? What thoughts, feelings, images, insights, sensations emerge when you image a feminine God creating human beings in Her image?

Does this description of the creation of human life from the muck of the earth strike you? Do you see a connectedness between human life created from the mud of the earth and the creation of earth's creatures? If so, describe this relationship. How can you appreciate and celebrate the beauty of this connectedness between human and earthly creatures?

6. As you reflect on these questions, what thoughts, images feelings, sensations, memories, insights are you aware of?

7. Record you insights, feelings, thoughts, images, memories, sensations in a journal, in art, poetry, song, dance or in any creative way you choose.

8. According to creation spirituality human persons are called to be creative and compassionate blessings for all of earth's creatures and all of earth's creatures are sources of blessings to humankind. The purpose of life is to return the gifts one has received by blessing other creatures, Mother Earth and the entire cosmos. Do you

see yourself as a blessing for earth's creatures? Do you treat earth's creatures with reverence and gratitude? How can humankind become a blessing for all of earth's creatures? How can you develop a sense of reverence and wonder for Mother Earth and the entire cosmos as sources of blessings to humankind? What can you do to aid the ecological movement in promoting awareness of the importance of safeguarding the environment?

9. Think about some practical ways in which you can become a blessing to other creatures, Mother Earth and the entire cosmos. Decide on at least one thing that you will do to make the earth a more beautiful place to live.

10. Record your answers to these questions and/or any plans thoughts, feelings, images, or sensations that emerge in a journal, in art, poetry, song, dance or in any creative way you choose.

Bridget Meehan   who are you, God?   marie-Celeste, O.C.D.

Who Are You, God?

I am the womb of mystery
I am the birther of new life
I am the breast of unending delight
I am the passionate embrace of woman
I am the emanation of feminine beauty
I am the Mother of Creation
I am the cosmic dance of Sophia Wisdom
I am the sister of courage, justice, and peace
I am the feminine face of God
you have longed to kiss.

(Bridget Meehan)

Prayer Reflection

1. Spend a few minutes in stillness. If anything is causing you to feel stressful, try to let it go if only for a few minutes. To symbolize this release of stress, open your hands palms up on your lap and visualize each anxious thought or feeling flowing out of your being through you hands and disappearing into space. Close your eyes, breathe deeply. You may wish to select a word or phrase such as "God," "Love," "Peace," etc. to help you become peaceful and centered.

2. Reflect on the different feminine images in the poem above. Are you comfortable with these images? Why? Why not? Do these images present you with a new way of experiencing God?

3. Select one image from "Who are you, God?" that touches you. Pray it over and over again allowing it to sink into the depths of your being.

4. As you reflect on this metaphor be aware of any new ways God is revealing the Divine Self to you. What thoughts, images, feelings, insights, occur to you?

5. Write a description of any images that emerge from this prayer experience or draw a picture of them, or describe them in poetry, song, or dance, or in some other creative way. Be aware of any feelings, thoughts, insights that you experience as you do so.

6. How did you grow spiritually by exploring this feminine metaphor for God? Do you have any new understandings of the deep mystery of God?

7. Pray for an awareness of how you can introduce someone else to the richness of feminine images of God. Is there anyone you know who might benefit from exploring some feminine images of God?

8. Think of one or two ways you can share the beauty you have discovered in your exploration of the feminine face of God with this person. If you wish to do so, make a concrete plan to accomplish this as soon as possible.

9. Do you think it is important for church and society to use both feminine and masculine images to describe the Divine Presence? What benefits would occur if church and society were to do this? What impact might this have on the issue of women's equality in church and society? List the changes that might happen as a result of using inclusive images to describe God.

10. Close your eyes and contemplate the feminine face of God you have longed to kiss.

Mothergod

God the Mother came to me when I was a child and, as children will do, I kept her a secret. We hid together inside the structures of institutional Catholicism. Through half a lifetime of Catholic liturgies, during years of Catholic education, from first grade through college, in my professional work in Catholic education, for fourteen years in a Catholic monastery, we lived at my inmost center.

This natural religious instinct for my Mothergod gave me a profound sense of security and stability. She was the sure ground I grew in, the groundstill of my spirituality. Yet we remained comfortably at home in the bosom of Holy Mother Church. My Catholic heritage and environment have been like a beautiful river flowing over my subterranean foundation in God the Mother. The two movements are not in conflict, they simply water different layers in my soul.

This personal vision of God the Mother, incarnated in my mother and her mother, gave me, from childhood, the clearest certainty of woman as the truer image of Divine Spirit. Because she was a force living within me, she was more real, more powerful than the remote Fathergod I was educated to have faith in. I believed in her because I experienced her.

Instinctively I knew that this private vision needed protection; my identity, my very life depended upon its integrity. But as she guided me as an artist, illuminating my imagination, her presence in my life could not really be veiled. She erupted in my imagery. And it is as an artist that I am compelled to reveal this secret life we have shared for nearly fifty years . . .

I draw and paint from my own myth of personal origin. Each painting I make begins from some deep source where my mother and grandmother, and all my fore-mothers, still live; it is as if the line moving from pen or brush coils back to the original Matrix. Sometimes I feel like a cauldron of ripening images where memories turn into faces and emerge from my vessel. So my creative life, making out of myself, is itself an image of God the Mother and her unbroken story of emergence in our lives.

(Introduction, Meinrad Craighead, *The Mother's Songs*, New York; Paulist Press, 1986.)

81

Prayer Reflection

1. Record the following directions onto a cassette tape, reading slowly, and listen to them, or ask someone to read them slowly to you.

Sit in a comfortable position or lie down. Keep your body straight, without crossed legs or arms . . . Close your eyes. Become aware of your body . . . Feel the pressure of your body relaxing on the chair or the floor . . . Feel the air flowing in and out of your lungs . . . Now breathe deeply for a few minutes . . . Become aware of your childhood images of God . . . How did these images of God make you feel? joyful? anxious? peaceful? fearful? sad? happy? Become aware now of your adolescent images of God . . . Were they the same as/different from your childhood images of God? How did these images of God make you feel? joyful? anxious? peaceful? fearful? sad? happy? Reflect now on your adult images of God . . . How are they the same as/different from your childhood and adolescent vision of God? How do these images of God make you feel: joyful? anxious? peaceful? fearful? sad? happy?

2. Take time to praise, thank, and love the God who was God for you at each of those stages of your development. Savor this opportunity for reflection and contemplation. Express your thoughts, feelings, insights in whatever form feels most comfortable for you.

3. Write a description of any images that emerge from this prayer experience or draw a picture of them, or describe them in poetry, song or dance or in some other creative way. Be aware of any feelings, thoughts, insights that you experience as you do so.

4. Reflect on Meinrad Craighead's description of Mothergod. What thoughts, images, feelings, insights, occur to you? Record your insights, feelings, images, thoughts, in a journal, in poetry, art, song, dance or in some other creative way.

5. Reflect on your own "myth of personal origin." Trace the story of your mother, grandmothers, great-grandmothers, as far back as you can. Get in touch with the spiritual journeys of your foremothers. Who were they? What did they look like? What were their hopes, dreams, fears, successes, challenges? What spiritual heritage did they leave you? Do you see these women as role models? Are they women you would like to imitate in some way? If so, what is it about them that draws you? Are you in the process now of sharing some of these same traditions with the younger generation?

6. As you reflect on the journey of your foremothers, do you see in them the living embodiment of Mothergod? Is it something in yourself they mirror? Are you aware of Mothergod dwelling deep within you? How can this image be a source of strength and spiritual growth for you?

7. Draw, paint, dance, sing, or find some creative way of expressing the journey of your foremothers, the heritage they left you and the images of the Divine Presence which they embodied for you.

8. Is there anything about the image of Mothergod that you would like to share with men or boys in your life? things you see that could enrich their spirituality?

9. Is there anything about the image of Mothergod that you would like to share with women or girls in your life? things you see that could enrich their spirituality?

10. Record your insights, feelings, images, thoughts in a journal in poetry, art, song, dance or in some other creative way.

Mother God

Marie Celeste, OCD

God: The Woman Who Dances Within Our Hearts

God:
The Woman Who Dances
Within Our Hearts

inside each of us there awaits a wonderful spirit of freedom
  she waits to dance in the rooms of our heart that are closed dark
  and cluttered
    she waits to dance in the spaces where negative feelings have built
    barricades and stock-piled weapons
      she waits to dance in the corners where we still do not
      believe in our
        goodness
          inside each of us there awaits a wonderful spirit of
          freedom
            she will lift light feet and make glad songs within
            us on the day
              we open the door of ego and let the enemies
              stomp out

(Joyce Rupp, *The Star in My Heart,* San Diego, California: LuraMedia, 1990, p. 61.)

Prayer Reflection

1. Sit in a comfortable position. Close your eyes and take several deep breaths, counting them slowly. Focus your attention on relaxing every muscle and part of your body, then resume your normal breathing pattern in a relaxed way.

2. Select your favorite piece of instrumental music. Read the poem above, imagining God as a beautiful woman who comes to you. She embraces you tenderly and invites you to dance with her. When you say "Yes" to her, she begins the dance of freedom in the depths of your heart.

3. In your imagination or if you wish to dance, stand with arms outstretched. Lift up your head and embrace your dancer God. Imagine that as you dance, you invite God to swirl, twirl, leap, stomp, tap, and sway through the rooms of your heart where you have experienced hurt, compulsion, bondage, sin and darkness. Notice that she patiently follows your lead, gently moving at your pace, stepping in rhythm with you into the rooms you wish her to enter.

4. As you dance, you begin to jump over some hurdles and stomp out some enemies. God's powerful love surges through you helping you to face some difficult issues, fears, anxieties and weaknesses. When you give up these self-made "barricades" and surrender some of your "stock-piled weapons," you begin to experience a liberation from sin, fear and bondage that you never dreamed was possible.

5. As this occurs, how do you feel? happy? relieved? peaceful? Spend some time sharing your feelings with God, the Woman who dances in your heart. Listen as God shares her feelings with you.

6. Continue to dance with your Divine Partner, swirling, twirling, leaping through the air. Experience the exhilarating love of God filling your entire being with a new spirit of freedom, healing and wholeness. The Woman Dancer gives you some special gifts to enrich your life.

7. When the dance ends, you spend time thanking the Woman of the Dance for these gifts. Listen as She thanks you for the joy and happiness she experienced as your partner in the dance.

8. Take time to contemplate the beauty of yourself as a new glorious creation. How do you feel? happy? joyful? excited? peaceful? What new insights did you gain into yourself as a result of this wonderful dance of freedom?

9. Has there been a time in your life when you experienced a process of liberation from any fears, anxieties, compulsions or addictive behaviors? How did this happen? Did trust in the power of God to heal you help you to experience freedom and wholeness? In situations like this do you think God, the Woman of the Dance, is a healing image for you? for others?

10. Write a description of any images, thoughts, feelings, insights, or sensations that emerge from this prayer experience. Draw a picture of them or describe them in poetry, song, or dance, or in some other creative way. Be aware of any feelings, thoughts, images sensations, or insights that occur as you do so.

Bakerwoman God

Bakerwoman God,
   I am your living bread.
      Strong, brown Bakerwoman God,
         I am your low, soft, and being-shaped loaf.
      I am your rising
         bread, well-kneaded
            by some divine and knotty
            pair of knuckles,
               by your warm earth hands.

I am bread well-kneaded.
   Put me in fire, Bakerwoman God,
      put me in your own bright fire.
         I am warm, warm as you from fire.
         I am white, and gold, soft and hard,
         brown and round.
            I am so warm from fire.
            Break me, Bakerwoman God!

I am broken under your caring word.
   Drop me in your special juice in pieces.
   Drop me in your blood.
      Drunken me in the great red flood.
      Self-giving chalice, swallow me.

My skin shines in the divine wine.
   My face is cup covered and I drown.
   I fall up
      in a red pool
         in a gold world
            where your warm
               sunskin hand is there
               to catch and hold me.
               Bakerwoman God, remake me.

(Source: Alla Renée Bozarth, *Womanpriest*, San Diego, California: Lura-Media, 1978, p. 166).

Prayer Reflection

1. Sit or lie in the relaxing warmth of the Bakerwoman God's love. Starting with the muscles of your face, tense them up and then let go saying "I am your loving bread," and surrender to her all that makes you uptight or tense. Continue part by part with your

neck, shoulders, chest, arms, abdomen, back, legs until you reach your toes.

2. Slowly read this poem several times. Let your imagination become involved in the rich imagery. Linger with one verse or stanza that attracts you. One or several of the following images may draw you:

I am your living bread.
   I am bread well-kneaded.
      Put me in fire, Bakerwoman God.
         I am warm, warm as you from fire.
            I am white, and gold, soft and hard, brown and round. . . .
            I am broken under your caring word.

Drop me in your special juice in pieces.
   Drop me in your blood.
      Drunken me in the great red flood.
         Self-giving chalice, swallow me.
            My skin shines in the divine wine.
               My face is cup covered and I drown.
                  I fall up in a red pool, in a gold world where your warm sunskin hand is there to catch and hold me.

3. As you reflect on these images, what feelings are evoked in you: joy? peace? wonder? gratitude? fear?

4. What strikes you about God? God's love? God's warmth? God's care? God's compassion? God's self-giving? God's hard work?

5. Did you experience any new insights into God's presence in your life? If so, did these insights bring you to a deeper appreciation of God's care for you?

6. God's love permeates the cosmos our earth, our relationships, our everyday experiences. How does the image of God as a Bakerwoman demonstrate God's active involvement in all aspects of our existence? What implications does this have for you in your contributing to the reign of God on earth?

7. How are you like the Bakerwoman God? What values, events, relationships are kneading, forming, shaping, baking in the fire of the gospel? What more could you do? What are your hopes and dreams for the future?

8. Share your reactions with God in loving conversation.

9. Record your insights, feelings, thoughts, images, memories, sensations, in a journal, in art, poetry, song, dance or any creative way you choose.

A Pregnant God Nourishes Us in Eucharist

If we are accustomed or become accustomed to seeing God through both masculine and feminine imagery, then the Eucharist takes on new meaning in the light of the most fundamental symbol of life in human experience: that of the unborn child who draws its very sustenance and life from the flesh and blood of its mother. (Source: original idea suggested by Sr. Kevin Bissell in response to a homily preached by Sonya Quitslund). It is thus only through Epimanander's image of the pregnant God and our understanding of the beginnings of human life that we can draw close to a truly profound understanding of the nature of the Eucharist and the intimacy of the relationship Christ sought to establish with his followers and offers to us today when he says: "Whoever eats my flesh and drinks my blood dwells continually in me and I dwell in him (her). As the living Father sent me, and I live because of the Father, so he (she) who eats me shall live because of me" (Jn. 6:56-58).

(Source: Sonya Quitslund, "In the Image of Christ" *Woman Priests*, edited by Leonard Swidler and Arlene Swidler, New York: Paulist Press, 1977. p. 268).

Prayer Reflection

1. Take a few minutes to relax. Close your eyes and breathe deeply. In your imagination you are no longer seated in your chair but you are in the darkness of your mother's womb. Relive the scenes, sights, smells that you experienced there.

2. Picture in your mind how your mother looked: face, hairstyle, body, clothing. Imagine how she felt as she became aware for the first time that she was pregnant with you.

3. Spend some time reflecting on what your mother experienced during her pregnancy with you. How did she take care of herself? Did she have access to medical care: What were her joys? burdens? fears? hopes? anxieties? thoughts? feelings?

4. Spend some time reflecting on what you experienced as you grew inside your mother's womb. Imagine the beauty of "you" as a developing fetus inside your mother's body. Observe how your mother's body provided all the nourishment you needed to grow. Look with wonder at what is taking place: the multiplication of your cells, the growth of your tissues, bones, nerves, the formation of

your organs, heart, brain, kidneys, lungs, reproductive organs. Experience the sights and tastes, feel the feelings.

5. Take time, if you wish, to record your thoughts, feelings, images, sensations that emerge during this prayer experience.

6. Now reread the passage above and reflect on the image of God as a pregnant woman who nourishes us with her body and blood in the Eucharist. Does this image give new insight into the intimate relationship we experience with Christ in the Eucharist? Why? Why not?

7. What thoughts, images, feelings, sensations occur as you reflect on the image of a pregnant God nourishing us in Eucharist?

8. Are you aware of any other feminine images of God that give the Eucharist new meaning? If so, explain what thoughts, images, feelings, sensations occur as you reflect on these images.

9. Record your insights, thoughts, feelings, sensations, memories in your journal, in art, poetry, song, dance or in any creative way you choose.

WomanChrist

WomanChrist spirituality incarnates a new image for living. Imagination functions as its power source and compelling quality. The image rises within and draws us to live out its reality—the image of peace, the image of compassion, the image of cooperation. Prayer becomes the living out of the image given. It is an extroverted prayer of creative imagination. It is a prayer living out the Christ-for-us, the WomanChrist. The images we live out are as many and as individual as the women and men who imagine, and they are collective as well. That out of which we live, incarnating it in our personal lives as well as in our world, is our prophecy—the manner in which the Holy speaks and acts through us in the process of creative transformation of the deformed world. In that living out we often appear mad. We whirl with a chaos that is dizzying. But as we swirl in the dance of the Divine Fool, we coalesce from the nebula to nexus, becoming a new constellation of life—a mandala of the human community, containing in its center the image of a compassionate God.

(Source: Christin Lore Weber, *WomanChrist,* San Francisco: Harper & Row, Publishers, 1987, pp. 133-134).

Prayer Reflection

1. Sit in a comfortable position, focusing on your breathing and relaxing.

2. Read slowly the passage above. What are your feelings as you read it? What strikes you about WomanChrist spirituality? Why?

3. In solitude reflect on the image "WomanChrist." Are you comfortable with this image? Why? Why not? Does this image provide you with a new way of experiencing and living out God's total love?

4. Listen to who WomanChrist is for you in this moment of your life. Be attentive to what WomanChrist wants to say to you. What did God reveal to you in this experience?

5. Is there an area within you or in your life that needs to be touched by WomanChrist?

6. What thoughts, feelings, images, insights, memories and sensations does WomanChrist stir within you?

7. Reflect on yourself as an image of WomanChrist, bringing Christ's loving presence to the world. What happens in you as you

experience the power of WomanChrist within you flowing out to others, creating a more compassionate world?

8. What thoughts, feelings, images, insights, memories and sensations emerge?

9. Share your thoughts, feelings, needs and reactions with WomanChrist.

10. Reflect on all women and men "living out the Christ for us, the WomanChrist," bringing about the kingdom of peace, justice, equality, and love to the world. What happens in them as they experience the power of WomanChrist within them flowing out to others creating a more compassionate world?

11. What thoughts, feelings, images, insights, memories, and sensations emerge?

12. Record your thoughts, feelings, images, insights, memories, and sensations in a journal, in art, poetry, song, dance or in any creative way you choose. You may wish to design your own mandala of WomanChrist.

God: A Woman who reveals herself in the Ordinary Experience of women

God: A Woman Who Reveals Herself in the Ordinary Experience of Women

"Who would want to prescribe how God should manifest him/herself—whether in a revelation to women in childbirth, in the way women experience the embrace of love, in the magnitude of a discovery, in the beauty of sisterhood, in their courage to walk upright?

Who would want to prevent God from speaking to us through different, new, old symbols? The spirit blows where he/she/it wills. Where life is being made possible, God cannot be far away . . . The way one experiences the female side of God, who like a woman in the parable lights a lamp to look for us, lost coins, God who wipes away our tears, takes us under her wings, prepares a table before us and fills our cup to the brim—all these images of the femininity of God are contained in the Bible, but they never entered into the language of tradition, least of all into the definitive statements of the theologians and philosophers; very few of them made it into the experiential knowledge of our prayers."

(Barbel Von Wartenberg-Potter, *We Will Not Hang Our Harps on the Willows*, Oak Park, Illinois: Meyer Stone Books, 1988. p 96).

Prayer Reflection

1. Take time to become aware of your body. Notice any tight or tense muscles. Become aware of any physical pain or stress. Become conscious of the emotions you are experiencing. Get in touch with them. What joys, affections, anxieties, choices are important to you? Don't attempt to change any of these feelings or thoughts. Simply acknowledge their presence in your life and affirm that this is who you are before God at this moment.

2. Invite God to love you as you are right now no matter how you are feeling or thinking.

3. Reflect on the qualities and traits that you value most in yourself? What qualities and traits do significant others value most in you?

4. Make a "What I like about me" list. And a "What others like about me" list. Post these two lists somewhere you can see them. Take time each day to read these lists and affirm your own innate goodness and giftedness.

5. Reflect on how you are the special image of God's presence to others in the ordinary experiences of life. In what specific ways do you mirror God's love to family, friends, co-workers, neighbors, associates? Make a list of "How I reflect God's love to others in my daily life." Post this list with the other lists that you made.

6. What qualities and traits do you value most in your significant relationships? How do these people reflect God's love to you? What are four actions or statements by which you can let these special people know what qualities and traits you appreciate in them?

7. How do you experience "the female side of God" in your identity? Sexuality? Significant relationships? Career? In the ordinary events of everyday life? Let God reveal to you Her Feminine Presence within the depths of your being and in your everyday relationships and activities. Be aware of any thoughts, feelings, images, insights that occur as God shares Herself in the ordinary experiences of your life.

8. Be aware of any thoughts, feelings, images, insights, sensations that emerge. Record any thoughts, feelings, images, insights, or sensations that emerge in a journal, in art, poetry, song, dance or in any creative way you choose.

9. Reflect on the following feminine images of the Divine: "God, who like a woman in the parable lights a lamp to look for us, lost coins, God who wipes away our tears, takes us under her wings, prepares a table before us and fills our cup to the brim." How do these images reflect "the female side" of God? Do these feminine images broaden your awareness of God's presence in the ordinary events of life? Select one of these images to meditate on. Be aware of any thoughts, feelings, images, sensations, insights that emerge.

10. Record your answers to these questions and any thoughts, feelings, images, insights, or sensations that emerge in a journal, in art, poetry, song, dance or in any creative way you choose.

Mary: Mirror of the Divine Motherhood

Into a world darkened to the mystery—miracle of Motherhood—
to a mind-set immersed in the genetic ignorance of viewing woman
as a mere depository for a male fertility principle, into this world
comes Mary, The woman of women impregnated not by man, but by
the power of creator God, unleashing that life-principle within her.

Into a man-managed world where woman functioned to furnish
the pinnacle of pleasure for male fulfillment; a world where woman
was called "provider of offspring" for the continuation of a male family line, comes Mary—the woman who needs no male intervention
for the offspring she will birth.

Into the gloom of unawakened awareness to the feminine-gift
comes the Offspring of the Virgin, the Savior sent to disperse the
darkness, to heal the blindness, to loose the shackles of consummate
ignorance.

The fruit of the Virgin's womb shows himself to be a lover of
women, a friend of women, a conversor and companion of women, as
well as men. In the midst of and in spite of the raised eyebrows
and rivet-sealed hearts of men of power, Jesus continues, publically,
persistently, eloquently, to befriend and to entrust with mission and
message the women who peopled his life.

All that time in the social evolution of humankind when the cata-
racts of vision had not sufficiently ripened for extraction by God's
restorative surgery, there came a woman and a man, together, hand
in hand and heart in heart.

Together they possess, this Son and this Mother, the magnetism
and charisma that captured during two millennia the imagination
and aspiration of thinkers, seers and dreamers. Each and both
generate a tenderness that "gentled" the more vicious extremities of
human behavior for two thousand years, until that time; until that
time when the integration of a developing human consciousness is
complete and impregnated with the Divine Vision of things.

The work they work is a mutuality of enterprise, still goes on in
our midst, and still incomplete moves yet towards completion. Humankind still wants for something and yearns for "Kingdom come"
with the Son who reflects the Mother and the Mother who mirrors
the Divine, each imaging the other in that indefinable merging-mys-
tery of the divine and the human, the human and the divine. Mary

95

has kept alive in human consciousness lest we forget, lest we forget—the tantalizing image of the Mothering of God.

(Regina Madonna Oliver, SSC M.A.)

Prayer Reflection

1. Let your mind plunge and sink to your heart. Welcome the womb-like enfolding that this restive center within your being offers your mind. It does not have to do anything. It does not have to wrestle with facts or conjure up ideas. You are restive and resting, supported and embraced, welcomed, loved and sustained.

2. Use the word: "Amma," "Mommy," "Mamma," oh so gently if your intellect, like a wiggling child, wants to squirm loose from this restful, welcoming lap of God in your center. The word (Amma) will quiet the wiggling child and allow you further time to relax in your love-center enjoying God's mothering.

3. After a few minutes of this contemplative experience, read again the reflection. Realize the providing care of God in giving us in the incarnation a mother-image that would and could span centuries. How would the behavior of human beings have been different if there had been no Marian influence" Has the position of Mary, the humble virgin and servant of Jahweh, become Mother of Jesus had a tempering effect on the world? Has Mary played a role in your life? Do you have positive or negative responses within yourself when you think about this? Can you write them down? Can you talk about them with God? With Use either paper-talk or verbalization, but be honest about your feelings, and about how you would like God to change you, if that is the case.

4. Had you thought of Jesus as a friend and companion of women in a world that relegated women to the position of non-entitites? Had you thought of Jesus' attitude toward women as reflection of God's vision of things? Read in Scripture the story of the woman at the well: *John 4: 1-42,* or of Martha and Mary *John 11: 1-44,* or of Magdalene at the Tomb *John 19: 10-18.*

5. During the week as you pick up your bible look for other encounters of Jesus with women. Read Luke's account of the Annunciation/Visitation of Mary *Luke 1: 26-56.* If you are drawn to it you might reflect on the Joyful Mysteries of the Rosary and notice any fresh insights you may have in light of today's reflection.

6. Do you sense yourself as being chosen for a mission by our Mothering God? What mission are you sensing? What is your answer to the invitation? What first step will you take in further

discovering your special task in the Divine plan? Write down your ideas.

7. Enter into a time of thanking and loving God who looks upon you with such special Mothering Love. Thank God for Mary in your life, in the life of the Church. Thank God for your own call to mirror the Mothering of God.

8. Let your thanks continue until it is a murmur of thanksgiving and restores you to that Center place where you rest and delight in the womb of God.

9. Before you conclude this time of prayerful reflection, record your thoughts, feelings, images, insights, memories, and sensations in a journal, in art, poetry, song, dance or in any creative way you choose.

(Source: Regina Madonna Oliver, M.A. Regina wrote both "Mary: Mirror of the Divine in Motherhood" and the prayer reflection that followed it).

Mary, from the Avignon Pieta   Marie Celeste, O.C.D.

God, The Laughing Spirit   Marie Celeste OCD

God, the Laughing Spirit

She is God, the laughing Spirit.
  Bright sparks of heavenly mirth
  Are bubbling deep inside her
  Just waiting to explode
  And shake me silly
    As I contemplate my own seriousness.
    She is a persistent God,
      Feeding my soul with heavenly food,
      Tickling and turning me
        Into a helpless hopeful clown
        Collapsing at the joke
          Of my own helplessness.

She is a healing God,
  Seeking my sorest grief,
  Finding my heart's fears
  And nudging me to see the humor
    In the darkest present moment,
    Bathing me in her laughing balm.
    Sweet smiling Spirit God,
      Keep the waters of merriment
      Simmering in my soul
        To spill from my clown eyes
        In warm, healing tears.

Release me from my stumbling sinfulness
And paint me all the wild colors
  Of your laughing rainbow.

(Source: Sara Muenster, Poet)

Prayer Reflection

1. Find a quiet, comfortable place to sit. Become aware of your breath as you begin to breathe slowly and deeply to prepare yourself to spend time with God, the laughing Spirit.

2. As you become quiet, close your eyes and think of a warm, bubbling natural spring welling up at the center of your being. This is the healing laughing Spirit that lives within you.

3. What other thoughts, images, feelings, sensations, memories or insights come to your mind as you reflect on the bubbling spring of the laughing Spirit God?

4. Think of the ways God "feeds your soul with heavenly food." Record some of these insights in a journal to become more aware of the nurturing, nourishing aspects of God.

5. Envision yourself as a "helpless, hopeful clown." How do you feel when you confront your own helplessness and what thoughts bring hopefulness to you in this moment? See if you can express these thoughts and feelings through art, poetry or in other creative ways.

6. Think of the darkest moments in your life, the moments of deepest grief. Were you able to find humor *somewhere* amid the sadness? If so, what did it do for you? Try to recall the times when laughter has been a healing power in your life.

7. What are the moments or situations that make you laugh, "strike you funny"? How did you feel the times you have laughed "at" rather that "with" another person?

8. Laughter is one of God's healing gifts. What other gifts of God's healing have you experienced in your life?

9. Think of the last time you laughed so hard the "tears ran down your face." How did your body feel after the experience? Were you laughing with another person? If so, did you feel a connection with that person through the laughing Spirit God?

10 How can you bring the healing of the laughing Spirit God to others who are hurting and grieving? Think of yourself as a laughing clown, painted in a rainbow of wild colors, giving thanks and praise to God and sharing God's laughter with the whole world.

11. Record your answers to these questions and/or any plans, thoughts, feelings, images, or sensations that emerge in a journal, in art, poetry, song, dance or in any creative way you choose.

(Source: Sara Muenster. Sara wrote the poem and the prayer reflection for "God, the Laughing Spirit.")

A word about the illustrations, by Marie-Celeste Fadden:

The cover is meant to illustrate the theme of this book: We are continuing humanity's ongoing, never-ending search for the face of God. The symbol of the "Great Spirit" signifies the beginnings of this search in all primitive peoples. This design was used by the Northwest Indians to designate sacred vessels reserved for divine worship. It is used throughout this book because it also hints at *our own* sacredness as the epitome of Creation: humankind—vessels that hold the reality that this symbol points to throughout our history. The map represents Creation, our only firm source for pursuing that search.

When God advised the chosen people about how to find their way back to the Divine Presence, the secret was given that we should look to Creation. And just in case we didn't have the resources to do that, God would place the "Eye of God" in our hearts, so that we could not miss. Working from that, we began to grasp what it meant to be created in God's image and likeness. We began to see that God was both masculine and feminine—in the *manner* in which we would each receive a share in the Divine manifestation of God's own life-giving force, which we often call "grace."

By reflecting on what it meant to be created in the image and likeness of God we discovered that *we also* have masculine and feminine poles from this gift.

Finally, we came into this world—and will leave it—unembellished with clothing. The human being was an expression of God's idea of the most beautiful, the most carefully engineered product of God's love. Thus, these drawings are not meant to be portraits of God. They are reflections on the meanings of this carefully researched text. We use the human figure as the most compelling example of what God meant when we read: "God saw that it was *good.*"

> Not in forgetfulness, and
> Not in utter nakedness,
> But trailing clouds of glory
> Do we come from God who is our home.
>
> —William Wordsworth

About the artist:

Sister Marie-Celeste Fadden is a Carmelite Sister who lives in Reno, Nevada. She was raised in a family of generations of artists, and continued that education in the schools of the Pennsylvania Academy of Fine Arts, in Philadelphia, and the Barnes Foundation in Merion, as well as in many other schools and various programs. She travelled and studied in Europe as a Cresson Scholar, and supported her own studio in Philadelphia by teaching, showing in galleries throughout the East and Mid-West, and winning a number of prizes. In 1950, her last year before entering Carmel, she was one of two Pennsylvania artists accepted in the Metropolitan Museum of Art's First Juried Exhibition. The other Pennsylvanian was Andrew Wyeth. While in Carmel, she continued her work, notably the mural and Iconostasis of the Russian Rite Church in Montreal, which she restored in 1988.

She continues to work as a painter, designer, and graphic artist in a contemplative community that supports itself in a Guild-system team that operates a Print Shop. Their ministry is to publish cards, booklets, and literary and artistic works of the highest quality, while adhering to a contemplative life in the manner of St. Teresa of Avila.